17.50

D0938864

College as a Training Ground for Jobs

Lewis C. Solmon
Ann S. Bisconti
Nancy L. Ochsner

Published in cooperation
with the Higher Education
Research Institute

College as a Training Ground for Jobs

PRAEGER SPECIAL STUDIES IN U.S. ECONOMIC, SOCIAL, AND POLITICAL ISSUES

Praeger Publishers   New York   London

Library of Congress Cataloging in Publication Data

Solmon, Lewis C
    College as a training ground for jobs.

    (Praeger special studies in U.S. economic, social,
and political issues)
    "Published in cooperation with the Higher Education
Research Institute."
    Includes index.
    1. Professional education—United States.
2. Universities and colleges—United States.
I. Bisconti, Ann S., joint author. II. Ochsner,
Nancy L., joint author. III. Higher Education
Research Institute. IV. Title.
LC1059.S64   378'.01'3   77-2939
ISBN 0-275-24450-4

        The research report herein was performed pursuant to grants
from the National Institute of Education, U.S. Department of Health,
Education and Welfare (Project Number NIE-6-74-0091) and the
College Placement Council. Contractors undertaking such projects
under Government sponsorship are encouraged to express freely
their professional judgment in the conduct of the project. Points of
view or opinions stated do not, therefore, necessarily represent
official National Institute of Education position or policy.

PRAEGER PUBLISHERS
200 Park Avenue, New York, N.Y. 10017, U.S.A.

Published in the United States of America in 1977
by Praeger Publishers, Inc.

789   038   987654321

© 1977 by Praeger Publishers, Inc.

Printed in the United States of America

Dedicated to the memory of
Allan M. Cartter

This book evolved from a challenge to the senior author, Lewis C. Solmon, in 1973 by Betty Vetter of the Scientific Manpower Commission that he write a paper explaining where bachelor's-degree holders take jobs if they are not working in the field for which they trained. The paper, ultimately authored by Solmon and Bisconti, was presented to the American Association for the Advancement of Science in February 1974. It raised many questions for which the National Institute of Education provided funds for more detailed analyses. In addition, the College Placement Council provided resources to conduct a new follow-up survey of the freshman class of 1961.

As the study evolved, related questions were raised in the pages of *Change* magazine, particularly by James O'Toole and Richard Freeman. The public media picked up the issues of underemployment of college graduates and the value of college education. The ongoing debate altered the focus of this book.

Visits to several campuses, particularly the University of Alabama, sharpened some of our arguments. It was a challenge to see if data-based research could be applied to the actual experiences of the colleges.

This study builds upon 15 years of work of our colleague, Alexander W. Astin, who has collected data on college freshmen over this period through the Cooperative Institutional Research program of the American Council on Education and the University of California, Los Angeles. Dr. Astin has supervised earlier follow-up surveys of the 1961 class, and his insights and encouragement have been a continuing stimulation.

Along the way we received advice, if not always consent, from Helen S. Astin, Don Casella, Kenneth E. Clark, David Goodwin, Ella M. Kelly, Jean Kessler, Harry Silverman, Dael Wolfle, the late Allan M. Cartter, and others. We have benefited greatly from their earlier work. C. E. Christian prepared the Index and made many valuable suggestions that improved the book.

Research and secretarial assistance has come from the top-notch staff of the Higher Education Research Institute, including Karla Kroessing, Paul Hemond, Pat Nelson, Jyoti Nebhnani, and Valerie Kesler. Beverly Watkins' editing has once again made our complex prose somewhat more readable.

Most of all, our thanks go to the group of 8,000 1961 college freshmen who allowed themselves to be surveyed for the fourth time. We hope this book justifies their efforts.

CONTENTS

LIST OF TABLES

College as a Training Ground for Jobs

A dual-pronged attack is currently being mounted against this country's economic and educational systems. It is argued that, "as part of a drive for profits and the accumulation of capital, managers in an economic system like ours endlessly divide, simplify, and eliminate jobs." However, more and more people are getting higher education. Hence, "the educational requirements for jobs have been artificially inflated, and access to jobs becomes an increasingly rigid process" (Grubb and Lazerson 1975, p. 472).

The educational system is accused of ignoring the alleged inadequate demand for highly educated workers as it continues to "lure" unknowing youth into a situation that leads to nothing but demoralizing low-level jobs. As awareness of this phenomenon has grown, it is charged that the educational community attempts "to attenuate this dysfunction by bringing aspirations in line with the availability of high-skill jobs, by replacing high aspirations with lower ones, and by preparing students in ways that make continuation to higher education more difficult" (Grubb and Lazerson 1975, p. 473).

Apparently, the educational system is a victim of the larger society. If it attempts to broaden the educational base of this country, it is at fault for expanding aspirations unrealistically. If it attempts to channel individuals into areas where their labor is in demand, particularly if these areas are of lower status, then it is guilty of trying to stratify society and reduce opportunities for upward mobility.

In a sense, higher education and the more general educational system are viewed by many radical critics as guilty of "accepting the economic system as just; it seeks to make people satisfied with their roles in a society that distributes goods inequitably" (Grubb and Lazerson 1975, p. 473). There is a feeling that the educational system is improperly preparing students to face the world of work.

1

A recent review of the transformation of society's ethic, in recognizing the decline of the puritan or the work ethic, has stated that, "As traditional value systems weaken, others grow in strength, some only temporarily." In the mid-1970s there is evidence of what might best be described as a "no-risk ethic," with everyone wanting assurance of what is coming to him or her and someone to blame and hold responsible if things go wrong. People increasingly want to be "insured" against job loss, family breakup, inadequate or incorrect medical attention, and unsafe or faulty products (*Culture in Transformation* 1975, p. 7). It is not enough that education increases one's chances of finding a job; it is now argued that students are justified in demanding assurance of a "good job" upon graduation.

From the recent rhetoric, some conclude that the value of a college education is decreasing, that Americans are overeducated. This observation is based on the declining rate of return from college education—compared with less schooling—over the past few years. Of course, this decline has occurred during a recession. However, the uncharitable iconoclasts writing from the Left see every fluctuation in economic activity as the precursor of long-term doom. Although fully aware that the economy has undergone peaks and troughs of economic activity for centuries, many writers now accept the most recent decline as secular. They predict that the current recession, unlike numerous others in recent history, is the beginning of a long-term decline in economic growth and development (Freeman and Hollomon 1975). They observe that the increasing education of the general population—something that most advocated only ten years ago—is evidence of an irreversible oversupply of talented manpower. This oversupply will lead, according to some writers, to discontent and probably confrontation (O'Toole 1975).* They neglect the fact that the college educated still earn more than those with less education.

Recent arguments may be summarized as follows: The system is turning out "too many" college graduates. Hence, they take jobs that do not use their college education; their earnings advantage over the less educated has declined (Freeman and Hollomon 1975). That is, many with college degrees have bad jobs and are underemployed. Hence, they are not satisfied and there may be a conflict between those 20 percent in the elite "good" jobs and the remaining 80 percent in the "bad" jobs (O'Toole 1975).

One possible solution put forth to prevent or delay the confrontation of the "reserve army of underemployed college graduates" (the term coined in O'Toole 1975) is for American colleges to stop producing so many educated people. This suggestion is attributed by O'Toole to an assistant secretary of

---

*An article entitled "The Reserve Army of the Underemployed" certainly implies confrontation in a Marxian sense.

labor, but is rejected by O'Toole since "other aspects of mass culture [also] foster higher social and economic expectations so effectively" that discontent could not be dampened by only closing universities and colleges.

The argument to restrict the production of educated people ignores evidence that many benefits of the college experience are not reflected by the match between major and job. It also forgets that most college freshmen indicate that to obtain a good job or high income ranks only about in the middle in importance among a long list of suggested life goals (Astin et al. 1975).

There are many benefits of college (Solmon and Taubman 1973), ranging from the enjoyment of a particularly entertaining class to the maturation acquired by dormitory experiences to greater appreciation of the arts. A more educated society is more politically aware and has less violent crime. These are only a few of the impacts of college. It would be a shame to ignore these and advocate reduced access solely because some graduates do not get jobs directly utilizing the content of their major courses. This point is acknowledged by some of the recent writers (O'Toole 1975) although it is too quickly put aside.

Most writers on educational and corporate reform assume that something is drastically wrong with what exists or with what has recently existed. The literature becomes self-reinforcing, as personal viewpoints are quoted and requoted and turned into data to become the basis for future radical policy recommendations. The most fearful aspect of the reform literature is its exceptionally weak empirical base. There is never time to conduct data-based research or controlled experiments. Those who possess the resources, both monetary and other, to conduct large-scale studies are viewed as part of the establishment—something obviously evil.

Some writers, in partial realization of the weaknesses of biased personal opinions, have attempted to provide "data" by putting forth juicy anecdotes. In the educational sphere, all radical writers know a taxi driver in New York City with at least a master's degree. With a heart-rending description of this highly educated individual who, after years of investment in his human capital, is driving a taxicab through the squalor of the East Bronx, even the least literary writer can paint a picture of the perverse nature of the higher education community in juxtaposition with the even worse leaders of the capitalist business community ("Slim Pickings" 1976).

Two additional types of evidence are presented to demonstrate the futility of college education vis-a-vis the world of work. First is the low-skill requirements for most jobs. However, little attention is paid to ways these requirements are determined. It is hypothesized in this study that the statement, "in the foreseeable future, more than 80 percent of all occupations will require the acquisition of vocational skills at less than the baccalaureate level" (Hoyt 1974), does not rule out the possibility that individuals holding these jobs who have more than the minimum required skills are fully utilizing their talents.

Jobs may be modified or expanded to take advantage of all skills of the jobholders.

Second are studies that show that educated people do not think their skills are fully utilized. However, these studies fail to recognize that most respondents to such questions as "Are your skills fully utilized?" base their answers on a broader set of skills than those acquired in college. Moreover, most successful college graduates may believe that they could achieve more than they do.

The defenses so far against those seeking to reduce access to college have been to note non-job-related social and private benefits of college and to deprecate the data of the challengers. However, since certain commentators believe that neither general nor vocational education has facilitated the acquisition of useful job skills and relevant jobs, some have suggested a new concept —career education. They advocate acceptance of education as preparation for work as both a prominent and permanent goal of American education. To achieve this acceptance, two changes in attitudes are required of certain educators and laymen: rejection of the notion that only courses and programs labeled "vocational education" are concerned with readying students for work; and acceptance of the notion that there are career implications in almost every course (Hoyt 1974). Career education should effect an awareness in teachers and students at all levels of the importance of education for job preparation.

In the rubric of career education, preparation for "work" has been broadened to mean preparation for "all conscious effort aimed at producing benefits for oneself and/or for oneself and others . . . whether such effort is paid or unpaid in nature" (Hoyt 1974, p. 2). That is, even part of leisure is work. This approach avoids the issue currently being debated. The changing definitions lead to changing criteria for deciding whether education is useful for work.

To redirect the evaluation: obviously, what is taught in college is more likely to be relevant to one's "work" than to one's "occupation"—primary work role in the world of paid employment (Hoyt 1974). Rather than broaden the functions for which college is expected to be useful, this study focuses on a wider set of skills useful in occupations (jobs for pay) than is traditionally considered. Which aspects of the college experience make better or more satisfied workers and facilitate higher earnings? What do individuals consider when they decide whether their college education is useful for or related to their job?

This study is more modest than many on this topic. It does not seek to change the world or to change radically the educational or productive institutions in the economy. The study was undertaken for nonpolitical reasons. It is an attempt to analyze old and new data on a representative group of the nation's citizens who are part of the labor force. The study is distinguishable from others in that its results are based on responses of almost 8,000 present-day workers who have achieved a bachelor's degree. This group is supposed to be leading the imminent revolution of the underemployed educated masses.

In 1973, the American Association for the Advancement of Science was concerned that, despite the large number of B.A.'s awarded each year in specific fields, there were far smaller numbers employed in these fields. That is, although a certain number of individuals graduated each year with bachelor's degrees in, say, chemistry, there were far fewer practicing chemists in the United States than the sum of those who had chemistry degrees would indicate. Hence, the senior author was asked to find out where all the bachelor's recipients went, if not into the field of their major.

Research by Bisconti and Solmon (1974) discovered that a large number of college graduates had indicated in a 1971 survey that they were not working in the field for which they had been trained. This seemingly obvious finding raised two additional questions considered in this study. First, what did workers mean when they indicated that they were not working in the field for which they were trained? Was this an indication that college education was not being used? What aspects of college training were useful in work? How closely related was the job to one's college major before college training was viewed as having had some value? Second, does all this matter? That is, are individuals better off in terms of job satisfaction or earnings if they are "using their college training," whatever that means?

This study attempts to do several things: understand which aspects of the college experience facilitate performance on the job and define "relationship of job to major"; ask why this utilization of college in work is important; discover what a "good job" is; and find out how "utilization" is related to job satisfaction and income.

As the study proceeded, the heated argument regarding the overeducation of the population and the discontent in the labor force came to the fore. Yet, the results from this study continually appear to fly in the face of some prominent allegations. To summarize subsequent chapters: the study finds that the great majority of those responding to the survey are satisfied with their jobs. Moreover, most workers think their college education has proved useful during their working lives, either through direct application or because it prompted personal growth reflected in good performance on unrelated jobs. Hence, we have been forced to enter the fray. The data are presented as they emerged, although this approach makes us look like apologists for the current system. But almost 8,000 workers who completed the questionnaire said that things are not as bad as some writers have claimed. This presentation should at least add a little balance to the debate.

2

OVERVIEW OF
CURRENT RESEARCH

A primary concern of U. S. universities and researchers in economics and education today is the relationship between higher education and the labor market. In view of the increase in college graduates and the corresponding decline in the ability of the labor market to absorb these graduates into the "choice" jobs that were available in the 1950s and early 1960s, higher education institutions are forced to reevaluate the role they are playing and should play in U. S. society. Some of the most salient questions are: What are the benefits of a college education for the individual and society? Can college students still expect to find satisfying places in the work force? Will they be able to find jobs related to their major fields? Can college-educated employees still find satisfaction in their jobs, even though the jobs may not be closely related to their college training?

Many people have had much to say on these topics. The relationship between higher education and the world of work has come under close and critical scrutiny by the president of the United States and the Congress. It is the recurring subject of pessimistic accounts in the popular press. Certain figures seem to stick in the public mind. The Bureau of Labor Statistics in 1970 predicted that a college education would be necessary for only 20 percent of the nation's jobs (Flanders 1970). Yet about half the college-age population attends college and, eventually, most do receive a bachelor's degree (Carnegie Commission 1973; El-Khawas and Bisconti 1974). A recent article provided the shocking news that 80 percent of all workers in the United States are underemployed (O'Toole 1975).

Very little is known about the relationship between higher education and work. Most information is either anecdotal or inferred from general statistics that provide only the most superficial view of actual happenings in the world of work. On what basis, for example, does the Bureau of Labor Statistics conclude that a college education is necessary for only 20 percent of the nation's jobs? That conclusion is based on the statistic that 80 percent of available jobs are in categories in which persons with less than a college education have been employed. But does the fact that a job was once held by a high school graduate make it undesirable for a college graduate? To what extent will college education be wasted in such jobs? To what extent will college graduates be dissatisfied? In his conclusions about underemployment, O'Toole assumes that college graduates and others will be unable to find work in their field of study. But do college graduates require a close link between their major and their occupation to be satisfied with their work? From a societal perspective, is education wasted if college graduates work in jobs unrelated to their major? Obviously, until these questions are answered, one cannot assess the nature and extent of the problems in the relationship between education and work or develop serious remedies.

THE PRESENT STUDY

The specific intent of this study was to find out, first, what college graduates mean when they say their job is related to their major and, second, to what extent and in what instances the major-job relationship influences job satisfaction. To examine these questions thoroughly it was necessary to learn the nature of the job, the content of education used with various degrees of frequency by graduates in particular occupations, the reasons graduates do not work in jobs that are closely related to their majors, the particular uses of college-acquired skills and the specific benefits graduates attribute to their education. It was also necessary to learn which college courses graduates would recommend for their own jobs.

The effect of relationship on job satisfaction and salary is examined, with separate chapters devoted to career outcomes for graduates in particular majors and particular occupations. This study is about wisdom—the wisdom that college education may or may not be injecting into successive generations of young and old adults, such as business leaders, educators, politicians, technicians, carpenters, fathers, and mothers. The study is also about waste—the extent to which college-acquired skills or wisdom may or may not be used in work and life and the consequence to individuals and society.

Approximately 12,000 graduates who had entered colleges nationwide in 1961 and had been working for up to ten years were surveyed for this study. The survey, sponsored by the College Placement Council (CPC) and the National Institute of Education (NIE), was conducted between November 1974 and March 1975. These men and women were part of a national panel that answered a freshman survey and follow-up surveys in 1965 and 1971 through the Cooperative Institutional Research Program (CIRP).* The original panel was a national sample of 127,212 men and women who matriculated at 248 bachelor's-degree-granting institutions. The 1974 questionnaires were mailed to all panel members who reported in 1971 that they had received a B. A. but no higher degree. These men and women comprise almost exactly half the respondents to the 1971 survey.

This particular CIRP panel was selected over more recent panels because, for the first few years after college, there is considerable career instability (Bisconti 1974). Long-run occupational differences among individuals are most accurately assessed after ten years in the labor force (Mincer 1970). The 1961 freshman panel had been working for up to ten years—the majority for eight or more years. Although it would be important to examine the influences of college education on early employment, the present study required more occupationally stable and experienced respondents to achieve a perspective on the relationship between college education and the labor market.

The decision to survey bachelor's-degree holders exclusively was dictated by the study's focus on undergraduate education. Persons who went to graduate school might have difficulty distinguishing between the effects of education acquired at the undergraduate and graduate levels. Moreover, one objective was to identify and explain differences reported by people with the same degree attainment. Finally, the focus of studies of career preparation, traditionally, has been more on postbaccalaureate training than on undergraduate education; this study should somewhat redress this imbalance.

The mobility of the panel necessitated special tracking to achieve a good response rate. In the first mailing, 3,500 questionnaires were returned as nondeliverable. Alumni offices updated 1,818 of these. Reminder postcards and second mailings brought the total completed questionnaires returned by the March 1975 cut-off date to 7,339, 61 percent of the entire mailing and 72 percent of those whose questionnaires were delivered—a high response rate for a mailed survey.

The sample was further limited to those who still held only a bachelor's degree and were working full time or had worked sometime between 1965 and 1975. Because of the small numbers of minority group respondents, the analy-

---

*The Cooperative Institutional Research Program, sponsored by the American Council on Education and the University of California, Los Angeles, is directed by Alexander W. Astin, professor of higher education at UCLA and president of the Higher Education Research Institute. The 1961 survey was conducted at the National Merit Scholarship Corporation. For a full account of the freshman and four-year follow-up surveys, see Astin and Panos (1969). The 1971 survey methodology and findings are reported in El-Khawas and Bisconti (1974) and Bisconti and Astin (1973). The career-related outcomes are further analyzed in three CPC monographs (Bisconti 1975; Bisconti and Gomberg 1975a, 1975b).

ses were limited to white B. A. recipients. The present analyses, then, are based on the responses of 5,536 men and women. A cross-validation study was based on the late responses of 278 panel members (about 4 percent of the full sample). This survey research methodology is limited by the potential for response bias, the collection of opinion-based rather than behavior-based data, the possibility that the 7,339 respondents represent a population different from the 4,661 nonrespondents, and the uncontrolled conditions surrounding completion of the four-page questionnaire. However, these data can help significantly in understanding the college-educated segments of the work force.

The polemics surrounding education-work relationships are so heated that even the most neutral commentary appears biased to some. For example, selection of the term "useful" is likely to evoke a negative response in many educators who do not conceive of knowledge acquired by education as a useful commodity but rather as the enrichment of human life and society. Nevertheless, findings of varying validity do support conflicting viewpoints on the key issues that disturb the higher education community and the general public today. The findings here must be considered in relation to the information and conclusions that already bear on the role of higher education, the college graduate in the labor market, and the job satisfaction of college-educated men and women.

ROLES OF HIGHER EDUCATION

It must be accepted that there are many benefits of higher education. Scholars in different fields typically focus on particular roles as benefits relevant to the theoretical constructs of their disciplines. The sociologist may consider higher education important for upward mobility of the lower class or for transmitting values, while the scientist may emphasize it as an institution to better the environment, the humanist to develop respect for cultural arts, the educational psychologist to change behaviors and abilities of individual students, and the economist to increase life income. Similarly, students, faculty, parents, employers, public officials, and manpower analysts all assess education by its ability to fulfill roles or functions that they, as individuals, consider important.

Preparation for Work

Many people believe that preparation for work is an important function of college education. However, among those who agree with this statement, differences over the meaning of preparation for work are striking. Some emphasize a career-education approach, which is essentially student-oriented although it carries obvious implications for higher education and society as well. According to this approach, colleges are obligated to provide their clientele—the students—with the knowledge and skills that will help them find satisfying employment, if they wish to work. Various programs have been initiated or proposed to increase students' familiarity with the working world, including cooperative education programs that make periods of employment an integral part of college study, work-study programs advocated by the House Subcommittee on Postsecondary Education (O'Hara 1975), and education-work councils proposed by the National Manpower Institute to involve the local community (Wirtz et al. 1975). Some institutions, notably the University of Alabama, have initiated comprehensive, multifaceted career education programs.

A principal focus has been career counseling. Most people admit that career counseling to date has not reached its potential effectiveness, due in part to lack of support by higher education institutions. This aspect of education has been given low priority (Hoyt 1975). Ineffective counseling is also due to failure of students to seek these services, which, of course, may be attributed to their low priority and low visibility. Bisconti (1975), comparing national data from various college classes, found a sharp increase in the proportion of students who sought career assistance from college placement personnel. Only 4 percent of the 1961 freshman cohort sought such assistance during their college years, but the figure increased to 10 percent among the 1966 freshman cohort and jumped to 25 percent among those who entered college in 1967. However, reaching students is a problem because, among all entering freshmen in 1975, less than one in ten planned to seek vocational counseling (Astin et al. 1975).

Disagreement about the purpose and content of career counseling is considerable. Some believe that students should be encouraged to make early career decisions so they can prepare better for a single career (Hoyt 1975). Others believe that students should not be encouraged to prepare for single careers; they cite the extensive career changing that occurs during an individual's lifetime, the possible future changes in supply and demand and skill requirements, the possible failure to find a job in a single chosen career, and the almost unlimited variety of occupations, many of which are "invisible" to students and counselors (Toombs 1973; Newman 1975). The latter group thinks counselors should encourage students to be flexible, helping them to become aware of their strengths and to develop these strengths as solid basic tools for a variety of jobs.

Some persons who consider preparation for work a primary goal of education think that the job market has or should have considerable influence on student preparation—the courses taken and the line of study pursued. As long as higher education is valued for its usefulness in the marketplace, it will remain as an important institution in society. However, as it declines in market value, as many people believe has happened recently (Freeman and Hollomon 1975), the American commitment to education may be endangered.

That this concern for marketable education has already influenced colleges and universities is evidenced in the recent curricular changes in one small, midwestern, liberal arts university, DePauw University in Indiana. This institution now offers a number of courses meant to be of immediate use to its graduates entering the job market. Reporting that almost half of each graduating class begins full-time work without advanced study, the university claims it is helping its students move into business, industry, and government careers with marketable skills (*DePauw Alumnus* 1975).

There is considerable disagreement on whether the manpower approach to curricular development is desirable or beneficial to students or the marketplace (Carnegie Commission 1973; Bowen 1974; Bird and Boyer 1975). The opposing views are apparent in the addresses given by Hauser and Newman at a national meeting of the College Placement Council (1975). Hauser recommended that government take a strong role in coordinating manpower planning and developing:

> Higher education has become a disaster area for a large number of reasons traceable to educational institutions themselves, to irrational dependence on our inherited frontier ideology and laissez-faire policy in respect not only to our economy but also in respect to the social and political orders; and to the growing erratic and uncoordinated role of the government. . . . Unless and until we recognize the need to increase planning and management mechanisms to supplement our market economy and laissez-faire policy ideology to cope with the problems of our highly interdependent and vulnerable society, we shall continue to exacerbate the problems which effect our nation, including the problems of higher education (p. 2).

Arguing that "the primary function of education in our country is not to match the output of proficient graduates to society's need for trained manpower [but] to educate students for a free and useful role in a democratic society," Newman warned against the dangers of "freez[ing] people into their slots." Noting that manpower planning has not worked even in Russia and Sweden, he predicted that the oversupply of college-educated youth will work itself out as the motivated and the achievers get the better jobs and society becomes accustomed to seeing college-educated persons in a wide range of jobs. He recommended "a return to a bit of Horatio Alger mentality," saying that "it's time we said openly, frequently, and forcefully, that going to college will not guarantee a job—of course, it is a tough world, it always was, but if one is interested enough and determined enough, there's plenty of opportunity around" (p. 16).

The views of those who consider preparation for work an important benefit of education depend on basic assumptions about the extent to which college education contributes to getting a job and to performing work functions. The first contribution may be largely through credentialing but the second relates to the success of colleges in imparting knowledge that can be used in work.

As reported earlier, the survey asked college graduates themselves to rate the usefulness of their education in these areas (Bisconti and Solmon 1976). College graduates think that college education has contributed substantially to their career progress, largely through credentialing, and has been moderately successful in imparting work-related skills or knowledge. In addition, both the credentialing effects and the function-preparation benefits carry over beyond the first job. Only 12 percent rated their education not at all useful in providing knowledge and skills for their current work, 38 percent rated it very useful, and 50 percent rated it somewhat useful. The first survey analysis indicated a qualified endorsement of education but considerable room for improvement.

Today, if indeed the number of college graduates is greater than the number of "good" jobs, the credential is probably more necessary or important than sufficient. When almost every new entrant into the labor force has a college degree, those lacking a degree will find it very difficult to get a job. Colleges can do little to maintain the value of the degree as a credential without restricting access, justifiable only if preparation for work is acknowledged as the sole purpose of higher education, but they can make greater contributions to student preparedness. Whether or not one agrees that this contribution should or could be made, many students do attend college for career-related benefits. Of all entering freshmen in 1975, over 50 percent stated that their reason for going to that college was that it would help them to get a better job. As an essential or very important objective, 50 percent want to be very well off financially (Astin et al. 1975). Of course, 50 percent of the responding freshmen had reasons for attending college and objectives not related to jobs and income.

Liberal Arts Education

Many different goals, mostly unmeasurable, may be included in the generic goal of "liberally educating" the college student. For example, some maintain that the college experience develops the intellect, changes values and attitudes, establishes certain interpersonal skills, and fosters leadership qualities. These outcomes of the educational environment are sometimes called the "external benefits" or "nonmonetary benefits" of higher education. One of the most important external benefits, if it is not acquired before college, is the ability to learn on one's own. Liberal education, then, is often considered learning how to learn rather than learning the content of any particular course. However, most advocates of liberal education would say that both process and content are essential.

The first analysis of study findings (Bisconti and Solmon 1976) revealed that colleges are stronger in some areas of liberal education than others. Although 73 percent of the students rate it very useful in increasing general knowledge, only 43 percent rate it very useful in increasing ability to think clearly. Just one in five give education high ratings for enhancing leadership skills or helping in the choice of life goals. In addition, less than one-third of the respondents reported that their college education prepared them for activities associated with traditional liberal arts and science education—writing and mathematical work. Apparently, colleges have been somewhat less successful in liberally educating their students than in providing credentials—a benefit that decreases in value in an oversupply situation.

Those who view preparation for work as an important benefit of college education may be disturbed that survey respondents consider writing and mathematical ability important work skills. In fact, much of what a liberal education professes to impart to students is considered valuable in work, especially the ability to communicate, figure, and deal with people. The responses of employed college graduates dramatically abolish the long-held dichotomy between liberal and vocational education.

Credentialism and Its Consequences

Most views on recent labor-market trends and their consequences for college students are pessimistic. While unemployment has received much attention, the possibility exists that underemployment is or may be quite extensive. Those who believe underemployment is widespread think that college graduates are performing work that does not require a college education and that they are not using their education on the job.

Some argue that in the past ten years the economy has not changed rapidly enough to accomodate the substantial increase in the educational level of the work force. Most educational researchers complain that employers have raised the educational requirements for most jobs, since the supply of educated workers is greater, without changing the nature of the jobs (Berg 1971; USD-HEW 1973). This imposition by employers of educational requirements not clearly indicated by the requirements of particular jobs has been called "credentialism," a term now used in a pejorative way (Gordon 1974).

According to Berg, the "rising demand for workers with more elaborate educational credentials, in the shortrun, is in response to available supply rather than to long-unsatisfied organization needs, and . . . developments on the education and employment front cannot be viewed with total equanimity" (p. 61). The most serious consequence of this arbitrary educational upgrading of job requirements is the displacement of a significant proportion of workers at the "lower" end of the labor force. These workers, who expected to hold jobs once held by people of grade school or high school education, now must compete with workers who have higher educational credentials (USDL 1972; Flanders 1970). The needless requirement of ever higher credentials for the same work and the failure of jobs to keep step with increased educational attainments have another potential consequence, according to some: the thwarted aspirations for the new work force. Although employers may believe that the more highly educated worker will be more productive, more easily trained, and have more self-discipline, they may feel the repercussions from dissatisfied workers, such as greater absenteeism and turnover. For many jobs, researchers have found an inverse relationship between educational level and job performance (Berg 1971; USDHEW 1973).

Many researchers (Taubman and Wales 1975; Chiswick 1973; Berg 1971) have questioned whether educational attainment should be a screening device for employment. One study of the relationship between education as a screen and subsequent income (Taubman and Wales 1975) concluded that American society has overinvested in education, especially at the higher levels. Berg found that data for blue- and white-collar workers are similar in that seniority is the main determinant for most promotions, although education tends to be a good predictor of starting salary and job title. Berg claimed that educational achievement is inversely related to production or job performance. With professionals and business managers, the more elite white-collar workers, the data become more complicated. Apparently, for those with less than a master's degree, salary is determined by factors other than educational attainment; for those with graduate degrees, salary is awarded by educational credential.

These studies imply that the jobs in question are performed as well by high school as by college graduates and that, consequently, the work does not require college skills. The survey findings do not permit an evaluation of respondents' productivity since respondents were questioned about themselves. However, the first analysis indicated that most think their college education does contribute to their work performance. Regardless of whether these workers are actually more productive than high school graduates, two questions are suggested by the finding that many work functions performed by respondents are not learned in college. First, does a college education provide a basis for learning new work skills which is more solid than that provided by high school education alone? Second, if not, why?

Although there is little question that employers raise their selection standards when there is a surplus of educated job-seekers and lower them when there is a shortage, some researchers (Gordon 1974; Rawlins and Ulman 1974) believe that credentialism is not as pervasive or as detrimental as usually implied. Gordon estimated that while 40 percent of the increase in the employment of college graduates between 1959 and 1971 may be attributed to educational upgrading, 60 percent is due to occupational growth requirements.

Are employers justified in upgrading their selection policies on the basis of education? Beyond the health and social service fields, few attempts have been made to analyze roles and functions in jobs, or to determine minimum standards or competencies required to perform these functions, or to determine what educational background provides these competencies.

Rawlins and Ulman (1974) emphasized that educational upgrading may be justifiable and efficient if the certification requirements match the employer's needs and if the increase in credentialed workers of the desired quality is overwhelming. Otherwise, educational attainment as a screening mechanism loses its efficiency and contributes to educational inflation.

Although educational credentials may benefit people and organizations, education cannot be accepted as an unqualified good, as in the past, without considering the consequences for both the credentialed and the uncredentialed in the work force. However, the data indicate that college students accrue enough other benefits from the educational experience and adjust favorably to labor market demands without totally sacrificing their ambitions. In short, an educated work force is a flexible work force. Educational attainment as a credential might be efficient in that education is correlated with many other traits desired of employees (motivation, perseverance, innate ability), it is costly to test individuals to see if they possess these characteristics, and the costs of testing exceed the costs of incorrectly selecting workers by educational credential.

COLLEGE EDUCATION AND THE LABOR MARKET

The relationship between college education and the labor market involves problems of supply and demand, overeducation and underemployment, and student and university response to market trends. Are college students unemployed or underemployed? Is this a permanent condition or a temporary problem?

Unemployment and Underemployment

The Bureau of Labor Statistics (1974) cited three types of underemployment: working part time, but wanting full-time work; having insufficient resources to maximize efficiency and production; and not using available skills. This last most concerns educators. Predictions that serious surpluses of college-educated persons will swamp the labor market abound (Carnegie Commission 1973; Warren 1975; USDHEW 1973; O'Toole 1975), even though long-term manpower forecasting is a hazardous business (Carnegie Commission 1973; Gordon 1974). One prediction states that, in the next few years, two and one-half college graduates will compete for every "choice" job, and some 350,000 Ph. D.'s will be job hunting (USDHEW 1973). O'Toole (1975) estimated that 80 percent of all workers in the United States are underemployed, precisely because they are not making use of their education in their jobs.

Our survey asked to what extent the respondent thought his job was related to his undergraduate major. Only 26 percent indicated "not related," while nearly 50 percent said they are in "closely related" jobs. Furthermore, only 10 percent think they "never" use the content of their major in their job, whereas 48 percent use it "frequently" or "almost always." In contrast, only 32 percent think their skills are fully utilized in their job. Apparently, although skills learned in college are used by a great majority of graduates, not everything that one learns in or out of college will be used in jobs at any one time or possibly ever.

Some researchers (Freeman and Hollomon 1975; Tussing 1975) take the pessimistic view that what they consider a collapse of the education and labor market relationship is a long-term change in the overall supply and demand balance, rather than a short-term cyclical effect, and that any attempt to increase the employability of the unemployed and underemployed through more education and skills will at best succeed in redistributing employment and unemployment, not in affecting the level of employment. Others (Carnegie Commission 1973; Fogel and Mitchell 1974) are more optimistic, believing that students and universities will respond to the labor market and make such adjustments as: self-selected reduction in enrollment in response to an unfavorable market; shifts in major fields in response to market needs; upgraded requirements for certain occupational fields, such as management and sales; creation of new jobs through structuring public demand for services and products; and reversal of the "brain drain," wherein college-educated Americans would be lured by better jobs overseas.

Student Response

Shift in Major Field

The data reflect two major viewpoints on student response to the labor market. On the one hand, the students are seen as quite responsive to labor market demands in their choice of major fields. However, their response lags behind the real events by several years (Fogel 1974). On the other hand, most changes in major fields in response to the market are seen as shifts in related areas (Gordon 1974). For instance, persons majoring in elementary education may realize the declining opportunities for jobs and decide to change majors. They then choose a related area, such as special education or educational psychology. Although majors in science and engineering have been sensitive to job prospects, the humanities have seen relatively small enrollment changes, given the disasterous predictions about job opportunities for humanists. The overall pattern of student choices and abilities, therefore, tends to be stable in spite of the relative "unmarketability" of people in certain majors. However, the case for student response to changes in manpower needs is stronger in graduate and professional programs than in undergraduate programs. In one rather unrepresentative study of 1,972 graduates of a southern university, 55 percent of the B. A. recipients who did not expect to find employment in their major field stayed in that major anyway, believing that it provided them with a wide choice of occupations. Some students (33 percent) stayed because they enjoyed the subject, and others (22 percent) learned too late that they had made a mistake (McCrea 1974).

In the past a stigma may have been attached to changing career choice; in a rapidly changing job market, flexibility may be recognized as an asset. Indeed, the replacement of old developmental theories of occupational choice (a limited decision-making period and a final, irreversible, compromising choice) with new sociopsychological reformulations (career choice as an open-ended process, continually shaped by changes in work and life, resulting in an optimal fit between career preparation, goals, and the realities of the working world) may attest to changes in career attitudes (Ginzberg 1972). More people are questioning society's demand that they make a one-career choice (Sarason, Sarason, and Cowden 1975; Campbell and Klein 1975).

Falling Enrollment

Will the increase in college graduates level off or continue (Berg 1971)? Unfortunately, past experience does not provide a reliable guide to the influence of a relatively unfavorable job market for graduates on the propensity of people to enroll in college (Gordon 1974). Reluctance to enroll during a recession may be related to the job market, but it may also be related to the ability of young people to finance a college education when there is such widespread unemployment. Dresch (1975) has argued that enrollments rise during recessions, since opportunity costs (earnings given up) are low for students who would face unemployment if they decided to drop out.

The Carnegie Commission (1973) suggested possible reasons for the change in enrollment patterns in the early 1970s: the increasingly high cost of attending college; changes in the draft law so it no longer deferred college students; the unfavorable job market for graduates with its attendant publicity; the shift away from academic programs in four-year colleges to more vocationally oriented programs in two-year colleges; and the greater flexibility of colleges in allowing students to "stop out" for awhile.

Gordon (1975) also cited several factors influencing the exceptionally favorable job market for college graduates and the high enrollment rates in the

1950s and 1960s which are lacking today. First, as a percentage of the relatively high gross national product, research and development expenditures to the colleges and universities were increasing. Colleges were encouraged to expand their programs, attracting more students. Second, employment increased substantially in the aerospace industry, which required many college-educated personnel, especially engineers. Last, a high birth rate prevailed in the postwar years and throughout the 1950s in contrast to the current almost zero population growth. The high birth rate, of course, positively influenced the teaching profession, in which many college graduates are traditionally employed. Not only are these factors no longer playing a substantial role in the job market, but it is also unlikely that they will play influential roles in the future. Although declines in first-time enrollment in four-year colleges occurred in the early 1970s, these declines were only among white men. Among white women and blacks and other minorities of both sexes, enrollment increased.

There are few data, but much speculation, on why college enrollments are down. One Canadian study (Handa and Skolnik 1975), with limited generalizability to the United States, addressed the influence of labor market factors on private demand for higher education in Ontario. Contrary to common belief, data from undergraduate and graduate students from 1950 to 1965 reveal that unemployment among the college-educated work force has a weak impact on enrollment demand. Expected earnings at degree completion, however, has a strong positive impact on enrollment, especially for graduate students.

Differences between the responses by undergraduates and graduates in the Ontario colleges to the market during that period are substantial. For undergraduates, increased umemployment appears to increase enrollment, but the effect is not strong. For graduate students, increased unemployment does not seem to affect enrollment. Although expected earnings upon degree completion are positively related to enrollment demand for both undergraduates and graduates, the effect is stronger for the graduate students and is influenced by changes in the ratio of average earnings of graduate-degree holders to those of bachelor's-degree holders. In other words, students appear to compare the advantages of graduate school to opportunities available in the labor force with a bachelor's degree only.

The question in the United States remains. Is this another temporary pause in the development of higher education, or have enrollments and expansion reached a ceiling (Bowen 1974)? Are the higher education institutions permanently tied to labor market fluctuations or is it possible and desirable to cut the ties and to emphasize other roles of higher learning? Because higher education is primarily financed through public and philanthropic funds, some argue that its future should be guided by public and philanthropic policy, not by the market (Bowen 1974).

JOB SATISFACTION AND EDUCATION

Although it is widely accepted that the increase in unemployed and underemployed college-educated persons leads to higher levels of worker dissatisfaction (O'Toole 1975; Berg 1971; USDHEW 1973), our data do not support this popular opinion. Only 6 percent of the respondents are "not at all" satisfied with their jobs, while over 52 percent are "very" satisfied. Even those who think they are in unrelated jobs or are not fully using their skills tend to be "somewhat" or "very" satisfied with their occupations.

Like much research in human behavior and attitudes, the study of "job satisfaction" is fraught with problems of definition. One definition is that job satisfaction reflects the extent to which a worker's needs are fulfilled through his job (Campbell and Klein 1975). Unfortunately, like intelligence, job satisfaction is defined by the test that purports to measure it. Sometimes the test or survey is only one question, such as, "All in all, how satisfied are you with your current job?" Some surveys contain more indicators of job satisfaction, ranging from "Would you recommend this job to your best friend?" to "How much is this job like the one you have always wanted?" Because of these variations, data from studies of job satisfaction are not comparable and must be interpreted with caution.

Job Values of the Bachelor's-Degree Holder

To determine the satisfaction of the college-educated person with his job, the researcher should first determine which job factors the person values most. Is the pay most important? Is it more important to feel secure in the job or to be challenged by its complexity?

Sex differences in the expectations of approximately 1,800 graduating 1972–73 college seniors were found in such areas as school selectivity, career choice, fields of study, enrollment in graduate school, and earning power (Gottlieb 1975). On the basis of this two-year longitudinal study of graduates from five different Pennsylvania colleges and universities, men are more likely than women to anticipate enrolling in graduate programs, while women are more likely to anticipate immediate, full-time employment. Although women graduates are similar to their men colleagues in educational credentials and job expectations, they generally expect lower salaries.

Regardless of sex, most students think they are quite different from their parents in that they are less concerned with earnings and job security but much more concerned with the altruistic and intrinsic aspects of work (Gottlieb 1975). Even though many students feel inadequately prepared for the job market, most assume they will eventually find employment with a reasonable income.

In a study of British undergraduates in the 1960s who rated certain pre-defined job attributes, Cherry (1975) found both sex and socioeconomic status (SES) related to students' ratings of job values. Although sex bears little or no relation to the first two factors emerging from the ratings—educational orientation of the job and relative job security—SES has a substantial relationship. Working-class students value job security much more than middle-class students. The educational orientation of the job is linearly related to SES: The higher the SES, the greater value indicated toward the educational orientation of the job.

The analysis of the last two factors—benefit of job to the self and people contact in the job—is much more complex, related to both sex and SES. Apparently, women are more interested than men in socially useful jobs that benefit others more than themselves. They also prefer jobs that involve contact with people. The effect of SES for men and women is quite the opposite: While upper-middle-class men place the highest value on an intrinsically interesting job that benefits them more than society, women of comparable SES are least likely, on the average, to indicate a similar pattern. Of course, these responses are from British students. SES and sex factors may have an entirely different effect on American college student ratings of job attributes.

When the survey respondents were followed up in 1971, they were asked which facets of a job were very important to them in their long-term career choice. Notable sex differences emerge in these responses to job values (Table 2.1). That jobs are available in their chosen career is more important to women than to men.*

More important to women than to men also are: originality in the job, the opportunity to make an important contribution to society, avoidance of pressure, the opportunity to help others, working with people, intrinsic interest in the field, and a pleasant past experience similar to the pursued career. More important to men are the possibility for rapid advancement, high earnings, prestige of the occupation, autonomy in the job, the likelihood of steady career progress, and the opportunity to exercise leadership abilities. Of comparable importance to both sexes is the opportunity to work with ideas. The opportunity to help others is most important to women, whereas the opportunity to work with people is most important to men. In a later freshman survey these sex differences remain much the same.

The 1961 cohort also differed when it related occupations and majors to job attributes considered very important (Tables 2.2 and 2.3). Availability of jobs

---

*These and the following data are based on a narrowed sample of 5,529 white students (3,124 men and 2,405 women) who entered college in 1961, received a B. A. but no higher degree, and worked some time between 1965 and 1975.

TABLE 2.1

Job Characteristics Important to Freshmen in Career Choice, by Sex (in percentages)

Characteristic	Men (N = 3,124)	Women (N = 2,405)
Job openings are generally available	25	34
Rapid career advancement is possible	33	7
High anticipated earnings	48	18
It's a well-respected or prestigious occupation	35	26
It provides a great deal of autonomy	34	25
Chance for steady progress	45	20
Chance for originality	49	52
Can make an important contribution to society	37	56
Can avoid pressure	9	12
Can work with ideas	51	50
Can be helpful to others	46	71
Have leadership opportunities	49	26
Able to work with people	56	70
Intrinsic interest in the field	44	52
Enjoyed my past experience in this occupation	44	60

Source: Unless noted otherwise, all tables have been compiled by the authors.

is most frequently designated as important to long-term career choice by those who went into allied health occupations and as least important by those in administration and sales.

Rapid advancement and high earnings are most important to accountants, administrators, and sales people, and least important to educators and social workers.

That the job be prestigious is most important to accountants and allied health workers and least important to social workers. Being autonomous or independent in the job is very important to those in administration, sales, and mathematics and sciences, and least important to those in allied health fields.

That there be steady career progress is regarded as most important by accountants and those in engineering fields, but least important by educators and social workers.

Originality in the job is valued least by allied health workers and most by those in mathematics and sciences and education. Making an important contribution to society is least important to accountants and most important to allied health workers, educators, and social workers.

Avoiding pressure is not very important regardless of occupation, with at most 14 percent in one occupational group responding that avoiding pressure

TABLE 2.2

Job Characteristics Important to Freshmen in Career Choice, by Occupation (in percentages)

Characteristic	Occupation								
	Accounting (N = 205)	Office Work (N = 379)	Administration (N = 780)	Sales (N = 364)	Mathematics and Sciences (N = 333)	Allied Health (N = 186)	Engineering (N = 294)	Education (N = 1,489)	Social Work (N = 185)
Job openings are generally available	34	30	20	21	38	55	31	34	31
Rapid career advancement is possible	42	21	43	44	30	11	32	4	8
High anticipated earnings	62	30	59	68	44	32	48	12	11
It's a well-respected or prestigious occupation	40	24	36	35	25	40	32	30	14
It provides a great deal of autonomy	26	26	39	42	37	17	23	22	31

Chance for steady progress	50	40	46	46	45	30	57	15	21
Chance for originality	33	43	52	45	58	27	49	56	39
Can make an important contribution to society	19	35	31	30	34	63	32	65	58
Can avoid pressure	5	12	5	7	11	11	8	11	14
Can work with ideas	35	43	51	48	59	31	58	55	35
Can be helpful to others	42	58	45	47	35	78	31	76	77
Have leadership opportunities	47	35	61	50	36	39	47	26	21
Able to work with people	51	65	60	67	43	68	40	73	76
Intrinsic interest in the field	31	44	39	38	58	59	52	48	54
Enjoyed my past experience in this occupation	36	37	42	42	47	61	40	67	60

TABLE 2.3

Job Characteristics Important to Freshmen in Career Choice, by Major
(in percentages)

Characteristic	Major								
	English (N = 515)	Arts and Humanities (N = 524)	Economics (N = 278)	Social Sciences (N = 1,071)	Natural Sciences (N = 627)	Mathematics (N = 311)	Business (N = 781)	Education (N = 640)	Engineering (N = 354)
Job openings are generally available	30	26	21	27	35	34	25	37	26
Rapid career advancement is possible.	16	12	39	20	20	22	40	6	34
High anticipated earnings	26	20	53	31	36	36	58	17	51
It's a well-respected or prestigious occupation	30	24	36	27	32	29	36	34	34

It provides a great deal of autonomy	38	36	39	38	29	27	28	15	26
Chance for steady progress	26	22	49	33	39	39	47	16	50
Chance for originality	61	62	43	50	49	48	42	55	46
Can make an important contribution to society	50	50	30	48	46	40	27	66	29
Can avoid pressure	13	13	6	11	10	10	7	10	7
Can work with ideas	60	58	47	49	44	53	42	53	51
Can be helpful to others	62	64	43	63	51	49	45	77	33
Have leadership opportunities	34	29	56	39	37	35	52	28	50
Able to work with people	66	64	59	68	48	58	61	71	45
Intrinsic interest in the field	57	60	38	48	55	53	33	38	49
Enjoyed my past experience in this occupation	53	52	41	47	49	54	43	70	41

is important. Working with ideas, however, is especially important to those in mathematics and sciences and engineering but not so highly valued by allied health workers.

Helping others is most valued by those who go into allied health, education, and social work, but least valued by those in engineering. Those who become administrators think leadership opportunities very important. Leadership is least important to educators and social workers.

Working with people is most important to many in the 1961 cohort, but the range is from educators (73 percent) and social workers (76 percent) to those in mathematics and sciences (43 percent) and engineering (40 percent).

Intrinsic interest in the field is very important to those who enter mathematics and sciences and allied health, and least important to accountants. The enjoyment of a similar past working experience is most valued by allied health workers, educators, and social workers, and least valued by accountants and office workers.

These data show widespread differences between the sexes and across occupations in those facets of a job deemed important. There are also differences across major field of study (Table 2.3). Compared with other majors, English majors place more value on autonomy, originality, and working with ideas. Arts and humanities majors, in addition to originality and working with ideas, find an intrinsic interest in the field important. However, they value least high earnings and leadership opportunities.

Economics, business, and engineering majors see high earnings, rapid advancement, and steady career progress as most important aspects of a job, and originality, making an important social contribution, avoiding pressure, helping others, and enjoying a similar past experience as least important.

Education majors regard the availability of jobs, a contribution to society, helping others, working with people, and a similar past experience as especially important, and rapid advancement, high earnings, autonomy, steady career progress, and leadership in a job as least important. The most recent CIRP Freshman Norms (Astin et al. 1975) show a declining enrollment in education which confirms the importance of job availability for education majors.

Overall, the most important aspect to English, arts and humanities, economics, social science, and business majors is the opportunity to work with people. Most important to natural science majors is intrinsic interest in the field; to education majors, the opportunity to help others; and to engineering majors, the prospect of high earnings. Whether a person chooses to major in a particular field because he values as important what he thinks people in that area typically value (advocating a self-selection process), or whether the major area itself influences people to value certain job aspects cannot be ascertained from these data. However, it is reasonable to suggest that there is some reciprocal relationship. (Sex differences and differences by major have been noted. Obviously, results depend upon the fact that there are sex differences in selection of major.)

Using a factor analytic technique to identify the basic dimensions of importance of job attributes, rated by a national probability sample of some 1,500 working adults, Quinn and Cobb (1971) found that five factors emerge: workers value comfort; challenge; finances; relations with co-workers; and available resources in their jobs. In a subsequent study (Quinn and de Mandilovitch 1975), educational level was found to be significantly related to only two of these: satisfaction with the job's financial rewards and the opportunity to find challenge and self-development in the job.

Many studies of job values have compared the responses of white- and blue-collar workers. However, Weaver (1975) has cast doubt on the efficacy of using these categories to index mutually exclusive, homogeneous groups of workers. As usually stated, white-collar workers are more concerned about the "intrinsic" aspects of their jobs, whereas blue-collar workers emphasize the "extrinsic" components, but Weaver has shown that the results are not so clear cut. In a study of white American men employed full time in white- and blue-collar jobs, Weaver found that the intrinsic characteristic of the job—that the work is seen as important and provides a feeling of accomplishment—is by far the most important component to both groups. The extrinsic characteristics—high income, job security, short working hours, and chances for advancement—are chosen by the two groups in similar orders of importance, but in these cases SES and educational attainment show substantial effects.

Chances for advancement are of concern to the less well-educated white-collar workers with lower SES and to the blue-collar workers who are dissatisfied with their jobs. Of concern to the less well-educated, lower-skilled white-collar workers with lower SES is job security. Those less well-educated blue-collar workers in jobs with less prestige are concerned about earning a high income.

Research has shown that those job attributes most important to workers are also those that receive the most extreme positive or negative satisfaction ratings. Consequently, many researchers who have studied job satisfaction have advocated weighting these ratings by job-importance ratings obtained previously. However, a recent study by Quinn and Mangione (1973) did not support the assumption that the validity of job satisfaction measures can be improved by weighting. In this study, however, the interval between the administration of the job-importance ratings and the job-satisfaction questionnaire was only one hour. This short interval could have biased the results.

It is important to know the workers' job expectations and desires to evaluate job satisfaction successfully. The educational background of workers may be a major determinant of their occupational expectations and, hence, their satisfactions (Berg 1971). Given this possible relationship, the Carnegie Commission (1973) rated, as high priority, fulfilling the aspirations of young people for more desirable roles in society. The question remains, however, whether researchers can deduce a worker's job expectations from his responses to questions on job satisfaction.

Job Satisfaction of the B. A. Degree Holder

A study of the relationship between college education and job satisfaction must ask: whether college-educated workers are more satisfied or dissatisfied with their jobs than less educated workers; whether college-educated workers are more productive in their work; and what the major sources of job dissatisfaction are. Although studies on job satisfaction proliferate, few have considered the variable of educational level. Furthermore, there is little agreement on the empirical dimensions of job satisfaction (Quinn and Cobb 1971).

A finding often given as indicative of an increase in worker dissatisfaction today is that an increasing number of people are going through a midcareer crisis leading to a change of jobs and careers (USDHEW 1973). This tendency toward a second career can be considered evidence of job dissatisfaction, but it can also be attributed to the rapid technological change in the economy, shifting consumer demands for certain products, and hence, the necessity for career-flexible workers.

In spite of widespread opinion to the contrary, a reanalysis of 15 national surveys conducted since 1958 (USDL 1974) demonstrated no conclusive evidence of a dramatic decline in job satisfaction. The analysis found that younger workers tend to be less satisfied with their jobs than older workers, but this has been true for the past 15 years. Possibly, younger workers have not yet reached their long-term goals, precisely because they are young, and therefore are not satisfied with their situations. Indeed, 44 percent of the men in our survey said their jobs do not fit their long-range goals. Of the women, 63 percent reported that their jobs do not coincide with their long-range career goals. We might question whether those whose jobs do not fit long-range goals may still be selecting careers, developing goals, and so forth. However, eight years of work is probably adequate to obtain a job fitting long-range goals. Most likely, those responding negatively are past the adjustment stage. They may have failed to get a job consistent with their long-range goals.

Even though most 1972–73 college graduates who were working full time when followed up one year after graduation (Gottlieb 1975) reported they are not firmly committed to their present jobs, they still indicated they are fairly content. However, many believed it would take additional formal education (the accumulation of higher level credentials) to fulfill their ultimate career goals.

Older workers also learn to adjust their expectations downward and become satisfied with much less. Job satisfaction may increase for people who stay on the job over a long period of time (UCLA Institute 1974).

Our survey suggested that the college-educated worker tends to be "somewhat" or "very" satisfied with his job regardless of the length of time he is employed (Table 2.4). The number "not" satisifed decreases only slightly over length of employment.

Next to the finding that fewer than 25 percent of all American workers are dissatisfied with their work, the most frequent finding was that job satisfaction increases with job level or prestige (Berg 1971). Indeed, most older workers would have higher positions than younger workers.

Our study analyzed responses to the job satisfaction and occupational level questions by sex. For three of the four level variables—sufficient job status, career progress, and professional level—both men and women responded more positively as their job satisfaction increased (Table 2.5). For instance, for those who said they are not satisfied with their job, 73 percent of the men and 74 percent of the women also indicated they do not have sufficient job status. However, 82 percent of the men and 78 percent of the women who are "very much" satisfied with their job indicated they do have sufficient job status.

For the variable "My skills are fully used," however, a different pattern is revealed across both sexes: Regardless of whether the respondents are very satisfied or not satisfied with their jobs, they do not think their skills are fully used. For those who are "very satisfied," the chance is only 50-50 that they also think their skills are fully utilized. This finding certainly does not support such writers as O'Toole (1975) who advocates guaranteeing every worker a position that matches his skills. No matter what the level of a person's job, he will probably still think his skills are not being fully used. But this does not mean that he will be dissatisfied with the job. Skills might be underutilized because a job is low level and less demanding than commensurate with the skills of the job-holder. However, there is probably a positive relationship between self-evaluation of skills and job level. Hence, those in the most demanding jobs might think their skills surpass those required by their job.

TABLE 2.4

Job Satisfaction of College-Educated Workers, by Length of Time with Employer (in percentages)

	Time with Employer				
Satisfaction	Less than One Year (N = 617)	One to Two Years (N = 700)	Two to Three Years (N = 658)	More than Three Years (N = 3,323)	Total (N = 5,298)
Not satisfied	14	7	7	3	6
Somewhat satisfied	43	43	40	41	41
Very satisfied	43	49	53	56	53

Note: Items may not add up to 100 percent due to rounding.

Although prestige is often an accurate predictor of level of job satisfaction, it does not correspond exactly with either salary or eduation needed to perform well (USDHEW 1973).

As our data show, even though women typically earn less and hold lower status positions than men, about two-thirds of men and women think they have sufficient job status and are at a professional level (Table 2.6). For women,

TABLE 2.5

Job Satisfaction of College-Educated Workers, by Job Level and Sex (in percentages)

	Job Level			
Satisfaction	Sufficient Status	Satisfactory Progress	Skills Fully Used	Professional Level
Men (N = 3,014)				
Not satisfied	27	12	4	38
Somewhat satisfied	53	42	16	61
Very satisfied	82	82	42	74
Total	69	64	31	68
Women (N = 2,179)				
Not satisfied	26	13	13	42
Somewhat satisfied	47	37	20	58
Very satisfied	78	78	51	76
Total	61	56	35	67

TABLE 2.6

Income of College-Educated Workers, by Job Level and Sex (in percentages)

	Job Level			
Income	Sufficient Status	Skills Fully Used	Professional Level	Total
Men (N = 3,087)				
Low (under $10,000)	51	27	46	99
Middle ($10,000–16,999)	62	30	66	46
High ($17,000 and over)	79	33	73	46
Women (N = 2,221)				
Low (under $10,000)	57	31	59	60
Middle ($10,000–16,999)	65	41	77	36
High ($17,000 and over)	79	44	86	4

feeling that they are at a professional level probably means they are low status teachers. Both sexes feel more positive about their job as their income increases. Again, regardless of income, most men and women are not fully utilizing their self-perceived skills.

Do B. A. recipients feel well paid for their work, compared with persons at the same job level in their place of employment and in other work settings, and with others with the same education? Apparently, the comparison group does not make much difference, although the level of job satisfaction differs slightly (Table 2.7). Overall, about two-thirds of the respondents do not feel well paid. The one-third that do tend to be somewhat more satisfied.

The Quinn and Cobb (1971) study of job values revealed six factors as indicators of job satisfaction: the five noted above, plus quality of supervision. Other sources of satisfaction reported in the literature are the opportunity for upward mobility and the relative deprivation of the worker when comparing himself to his education and skill reference group (Berg 1971). According to Kornhauser (1965), the perception that the job does or does not give the worker the opportunity to use his skills is one of the strongest influences. Others are the perception of the job as interesting or uninteresting and worthwhile or useless.

Intrinsic content of the job, not income, contributes most to job satisfaction among most workers. Rigid routine work leads to greater dissatisfaction, while variety, autonomy, and meaningful responsibility promote job satisfaction (USDHEW 1973).

Of the survey respondents who indicated as freshmen that such factors are important, most are very satisfied in their jobs (Table 2.8). If the somewhat satisfied workers are included, the group includes more than 90 percent. One can conclude that the vast majority of B. A. recipients find jobs that meet their most important criteria.

In Gottlieb's (1975) study, although the majority are satisfied with their full-time jobs one year after graduation, the gap between reported salaries and

TABLE 2.7

Job Satisfaction of College-Educated Workers Who Feel Well Paid
Compared with Others of Same Job Level or Same Education
(in percentages)

	Well-paid Compared with:			
Satisfaction	Persons of Same Job Level and with Same Employer	Persons of Same Job Level and with Different Employer	People in General with Same Education	Total
Not satisfied	25	28	24	4
Somewhat satisfied	32	29	28	41
Very satisfied	40	43	45	55
Total	36	36	37	(N=5,193)

TABLE 2.8

Job Characteristics Important to Freshmen, by Job Satisfaction of College-Educated Workers (in percentages)

	Satisfaction		
Characteristic	Not Satisfied	Satisfied	Very Satisfied
Job openings are generally available	7	44	49
Rapid career advancement is possible	5	36	59
High anticipated earnings	5	39	56
It's a well-respected or prestigious occupation	4	37	59
It provides a great deal of autonomy	7	41	53
Chance for steady progress	5	40	55
Chance for originality	6	41	53
Can make important contribution to society	5	40	55
Can avoid pressure	10	49	41
Can work with ideas	6	40	54
Can be helpful to others	6	40	54
Have leadership opportunities	4	37	59
Able to work with people	5	39	56
Intrinsic interest in the field	6	42	52
Enjoyed my past experience in this occupation	4	36	60

prior expectations is significant. This discrepancy is greatest, of course, for men, since they hold higher income expectations.

Speculation holds that when workers feel trapped and dissatisfied, they demonstrate lower productivity (USDHEW 1973). Berg (1971) and Henle (1975) pointed out, however, that satisfied workers are sometimes more and sometimes less productive than their dissatisfied counterparts, thereby giving no conclusive support to the assumption. The contradictory evidence may result from heterogeneous groups of workers assumed to be homogeneous, or it may be an artifact of the methods that assess satisfaction and productivity. No convincing data support a direct cause-effect relationship between job satisfaction and productivity. Whatever contribution satisfaction makes to productivity, it is probably indirect, such as reduced turnover, absenteeism, theft, and the like (USDL 1974).

Although the research on turnover is poor, the usual finding is a significant inverse relationship between satisfaction and turnover rates for better and less educated workers (Berg 1971). That is, the better educated worker is less satisfied and more prone to leave a job after shorter intervals.

For blue-collar workers, Berg confirmed that the better educated the worker, the higher his aspirations. In turn, the higher the aspirations, the more intensely the "effects" of education contribute to job dissatisfaction, although the relationship between education and satisfaction is rather weak. Skill levels consistently reveal a positive, linear relationship with job satisfaction. As job skill level increases, so does job satisfaction. Most satisfied, then, are less educated workers who think they have a high-skill job. Next are the better educated with high-skill jobs, then the less educated with low-skill jobs. Least satisfied are the better educated who think they are in low-skill jobs.

The discrepancy between the worker's expectations or aspirations and his actual job level is the most important factor in determining job satisfaction, according to Berg. Therefore, he concludes that if employers hire better educated workers for a "pool of promotable people," they may be generating discontent among better educated, aspiring workers placed in low-skill jobs, particularly where workers perceive relatively little chance for advancement.

Actually, the relationship between job satisfaction and advancement is somewhat more complex (Table 2.9). Regardless of occupation, dissatisfied workers tend to say their chances for advancement are poor. However, occupational differences at the other end of the scale are substantial. All but four occupational groups that indicate "very" satisfied concomitantly indicate good prospects for advancement. The four occupational groups that, regardless of job satisfaction level, think advancement possibilities are not good are allied health, education, social work, and other nonprofessional fields. Women, more than men, are likely to enter these occupations.

With data from four Gallup polls—1963 to 1969—Weaver (1974) found skill level a more significant determinant of job satisfaction than level of educational attainment. Even stronger is the association between the worker's satisfaction with his income and satisfaction with the job. Level of job satisfaction is considerably lower for black than for white men. Ash (1972) found that white women are the most satisfied, followed by Spanish-surnamed women. Least satisfied are black women. The Ash study, however, is far from representative, since the sample was quite small and all respondents worked in the same organization.

A more extensive study of the relationship between undergraduate education and job satisfaction surveyed a national sample from two freshman cohorts, 1961 and 1966, which was followed up by a 1971 survey (Bisconti and Gomberg 1975a), from which our 1974 group was selected. This study showed that the majority of the bachelor's recipients in 1961 thought their job was a "good one." Among the most satisfied are the education, economics, and language majors. Least satisfied are the biological science majors. Even in this group, 65 percent of men and 70 percent of women think their jobs are "good."

In the 1966 cohort, the B.A. recipients were less likely to think their job was good. That about 33 percent do not like their work may reflect actual differences in the two cohorts influenced by respective job markets, or, more importantly, differences in time on the job. The 1966 cohort would probably have been working at least five years less than the 1961 cohort. Again, education

TABLE 2.9

Job Satisfaction of College-Educated Workers and Their Future Prospects for Advancement, by Occupation (in percentages)

Satisfaction	Job Offers Good Future Prospects for Further Advancement, by Occupation										
	Account-ing	Office Work	Admini-stration	Sales	Mathe-matical Sciences	Allied Health	Engi-neering	Educa-tion	Social Work	Other Profes-sional	Other Non-profes-sional
Not satisfied	0	10	12	12	0	0	11	10	0	17	17
Somewhat satisfied	57	43	50	62	46	16	47	9	15	43	27
Very satisfied	80	80	77	75	75	48	79	28	30	74	48

majors are the most satisfied, followed this time by language majors. The least content are men who majored in such fields as psychology and history. Although satisfied workers are found in all occupations and women workers in menial and repetitive jobs are more satisfied than others in challenging positions, some researchers still assume that no one can or, perhaps, should find satisfaction in work they themselves would be certain to avoid (O'Toole 1975; Hoppock 1975).

Job Redesign

While it is important to know whether workers are satisfied with their jobs and what characteristics separate the satisfied from the dissatisfied, the current press emphasis on job satisfaction may have clouded a fundamental issue: Should the existing work organization and jobs be changed or redesigned? Is it possible to redesign most jobs to promote greater satisfaction? Should job satisfaction be guaranteed to all workers?

In advocating the "humanization of work," USDHEW report (1973) is considered by some critics (Wool 1975; Kaplan 1975) to overgeneralize the nature and extent of worker dissatisfaction and to rely too heavily on the potential for work redesign as a primary solution. For these critics, the most important improvements in the quality of working life in America are those designed to increase the quantity of work (Wool 1975). High employment rates, rather than more amenable working conditions, are a more effective alternative to upgrading the status of workers in low-level jobs and promoting equality of employment opportunity.

After all, how can one better match workers to jobs when one does not know how to assess their "dynamic psychic needs" or how to match these unassessable needs to job requirements? This criticism seems a little harsh and unrealistic. No one would try to match every specific need of every worker to the respective requirements of a job. But there may be some general psychological needs of workers which can be fulfilled by jobs generally considered unsatisfying.

Research on the quality of working life and job design has attempted to determine just that. When the characteristics of jobs allow workers to be largely autonomous and adaptive and to learn on the job, to have variety in their work, and to participate in the decisions affecting that work, then meaningfulness, satisfaction, and learning increase significantly (Davis 1972). Simultaneously, quantity and quality of production or service increase at all levels of organization and in vastly different settings, such as coal mining, chemical refining, and aircraft instrument manufacturing.

Probably no one change in a job situation would substantially increase satisfaction because the average worker looks for many things from each job.

But if one knew what the average person values in a working situation, it might be possible to redesign jobs accordingly. Although there is a problem with the design of work, it may not be of great significance (Levitan and Johnston 1975).

According to Hoppock (1975), it is possible to raise the level of satisfaction for workers. He has suggested many ways: helping dissatisfied workers to change jobs; studying the relationship between job satisfaction and working conditions to propose feasible changes in working conditions; helping students and counselees to learn more about the jobs they are interested in which might be open; advising students before they make career choices to consider which jobs society may be willing to let them fill; teaching students to have realistic expectations; and discovering the causal links between job satisfaction and its associated variables.

Should employers be concerned about job dissatisfaction? Should they try to increase satisfaction? Contrary to the USDHEW report (1973), work may not be a "central life interest" of all workers (Kaplan 1975). Considerable sociological evidence has indicated that workers can be satisfied in what some might consider dull, repetitive, meaningless jobs.

Perhaps it is not in the best interests of workers to be satisfied 100 percent of the time (USDL 1974). Complete satisfaction may induce complacency and inability or unwillingness to adjust to changing job demands. Perhaps dissatisfaction to a degree is a safeguard against these evils and a catalyst for flexibility. Perhaps job satisfaction is not important if a worker is satisfied with life in general. In this case, those about to embark on careers must be informed that their education does not guarantee them total satisfaction at every stage. A major cause of existing dissatisfaction may be the inflated expectations of students in the 1950s and 1960s.

JOB SATISFACTION AND LIFE SATISFACTION

The two most popular theories on the relationship between job satisfaction and general satisfaction with life are the compensation theory and the spillover theory. With the first, time away from work—leisure time—may become not only distraction from but also compensation for the worker's loss of interest in the job (Dumazedier and Latouche 1962). In other words, a dissatisfied worker may tend to compensate for his dissatisfaction through leisure-time activities.

The evidence, however, favors the spillover theory: The worker's feelings about the job will generalize to his other life roles (USDL 1974). A large-scale investigation of the mental health of U.S. auto workers in the 1950s (Kornhauser 1965) found that those workers who express job dissatisfaction are also unhappy with their lives in general. This finding supports a spillover rather than a compensatory relationship between job and life attitudes.

This study also revealed substantial mental health differences among occupations. Auto workers in the more skilled, responsible, and varied jobs have better mental health. This relationship between job and mental health appears to be quite genuine, not dependent on the selection effects of differences in prejob background or the personalities of workers who entered and remained in several types of work. The job affects the psychological health of the worker, rather than vice versa.

Job satisfaction is influenced not only by occupational level, but also by characteristics of the place of employment (Kornhauser 1965). Size of the organization is clearly related to mental health: the larger the establishment, the poorer the workers' mental health. Establishments that rank lower in mental health also tend to have a larger proportion of workers at lower levels of skilled jobs and educational attainment. In our study of college-educated workers, however, organizational size makes little difference in job satisfaction, although the direction of the difference is consistent with earlier work. All size organizations have more satisfied than unsatisfied employees (Table 2.10).

Although methodologically flawed, a study of the job satisfaction and life satisfaction of first-level supervisors from different departments in a large southern chemical plant has also supported the spillover hypothesis (Iris and Barrett 1972). Sample A includes 34 men who are four years younger, have about four years less time with the company, and are paid approximately $130 a month less than the 35 men in Sample B. Sample A is less satisfied with the job and life in general than Sample B. Confounding the differences in age, experience, and pay between the two samples, the researchers indicated that, in an unsatisfying job situation, satisfaction with pay becomes the major determinant of job satisfaction but, in a more favorable job situation, satisfaction with pay tends to be unrelated to general job satisfaction. In the favorable job situation, promotion opportunities and relations with co-workers and supervisors seem more related to job satisfaction and life satisfaction.

TABLE 2.10

Job Satisfaction of College-Educated Workers by Size of Employer (in percentages)

| | Size of Employer | | |
| | Under 50 Employees | 50–4,999 Employees | Over 5,000 Employees |
Satisfaction			
Not satisfied	6	5	6
Somewhat satisfied	36	44	41
Very satisfied	58	51	54

Only one study—by Kohn and Schooler (1973)—empirically appraised the reciprocal effects of the worker on the job and the job on the worker. About 3,000 men employed in different civilian occupations were interviewed by the National Opinion Research Center. Controlling for educational level and occupational conditions, the researchers found a correlation of .41 between job conditions and psychological functioning which they think large enough for serious consideration. Three components of the job have a significant relationship with the psychological functioning of the worker: closeness of supervision, routine of the work, and substantive complexity of the job—the most important component.

Income, occupational status, social selectivity in recruitment and retention of employees, occupational self-selection, and job molding bear little significance to the relationship between job conditions and psychological functioning in general.

Employing the "two-stage least squares" multiple regression technique, Kohn and Schooler (1973) confirmed that the relationship between the substantive complexity of the current job and psychological flexibility is reciprocal. That is, in their current reciprocal relationship, the impact of the job on intellectual flexibility is greater than the reverse. Therefore, the substantive complexity of the job is consistently more important for psychological functioning than is psychological functioning for the substantive complexity of the job. Whether this relationship is true for the job as a whole is unknown, but in the continuing interplay between worker and job, the effects of the job on the worker are far from trivial.

These findings support the spillover, rather than the compensatory model of the relationship between job and life satisfaction. The worker's ways of coping with the realities of the job seem to generalize to nonoccupational realities. For example, workers whose jobs require intellectual flexibility not only use their intellectual skills on the job but also engage in intellectually demanding leisure-time activities.

These data do not imply that workers turn their job frustrations loose on their off-the-job lives or that they attempt to compensate in their leisure time for certain voids in their jobs. That a worker's job affects his general perceptions, values, and thinking processes supports changes to make dissatisfying jobs more satisfying. Any effort to enhance job satisfaction and eliminate job dissatisfaction should focus on job redesign rather than other alternatives.

The Kohn and Schooler study only investigated the responses of men. A questionnaire completed by 93 civil service employees in office-type occupations in a large midwestern city revealed no significant relationship between job satisfaction and life satisfaction for women but a significant relationship for men (Brayfield, Wells, and Strats 1957). The job may play a more significant role in the lives of men than of women. When the job is important in the whole life scheme, perhaps life satisfaction becomes more a function of job satisfaction. Typically, the men in this sample hold higher level positions and are older than the women, two facts that confound the data. Higher level jobs may mean "more" or something "different" to any worker, regardless of sex.

In a study of sex differences in job and life satisfaction (Greenhaus 1974), 203 undergraduates at two eastern colleges indicated their attitudes toward their lives in general and their preferences in job outcomes. Men and women show similar correlations between life satisfaction and satisfaction with job preference. Life satisfaction for those who value success and rapid advancement is more highly related to satisfaction with occupational preference than for those who place less importance on these outcomes. Of course, educational similarity may have wiped out sex differences.

How widespread are job and life dissatisfaction? A 1972–73 follow-up of a 1969–70 survey of a national sample of 1,500 employed adult men in the United States revealed that 52 percent are "very satisfied with their current jobs," while only 7 percent are "not very satisfied" with the way they are "spending [their] life these days" (Quinn and Shepard 1974). More than 70 percent are "pretty satisfied" with life in general, but only 22 percent find life "completely satisfying." Any problem today with U.S. workers' dissatisfaction with their work and their lives is modest in degree. The greater proportion of dissatisfied workers think they are not challenged by their work and are not using their skills. Therefore, our concern should be with this subgroup; the major part is probably college-trained workers who are underemployed or in jobs unrelated to their college majors.

THE B.A. AND THE CONCEPT OF RELATIONSHIP

About 33 percent of men and 67 percent of women college graduates have had to accept jobs unrelated to their college majors in the 1970s, compared with only 10 percent of men and 13 percent of women in the early 1960s (Freeman and Hollomon 1975). When surveyed one year after graduation, many with full-time jobs stated that they are unable to find work closely related to their college major (Gottlieb 1975). Less than one-third, in fact, think that current employment offers opportunities coinciding with their original long-range career goal.

A limited survey of 299 technical and nontechnical employees from two firms investigated the relationship between college education and job position (Rawlins and Ulman 1974). That 50 percent of the workers in technical fields, compared with 45 percent in nontechnical fields, think their position is significantly related to college education, and that 19 percent, compared with 10 percent, think their position is very closely related, indicates that those who hold less technical positions see less relationship between their education and their work. Table 2.11 corroborates this finding. Almost 70

TABLE 2.11

Relationship of College Major to Job,
by Type of Occupation (in percentages)

| | Occupation | |
| | Technical | Nontechnical |
Relationship	(N = 2,744)	(N = 2,027)
Not related	12	39
Somewhat related	19	31
Closely related	69	30

percent of those in technical occupations, but only 30 percent of those in nontechnical occupations, think their jobs are closely related to their major.

Once hired, most employees, regardless of technical or nontechnical positions, think education is not very important to their careers. Such personality attributes as willingness to make decisions and to accept responsibility are more necessary to occupational success than command of specific skills that can be acquired through in-service training. Formal education may serve the employer primarily as a screening device.

Most men and women B.A. recipients in 1971 (ten years after college entry) were in business-related and teaching careers, according to a national survey (Bisconti and Solmon 1974). Of the teachers, most think their work is related to their college training. However, a substantial number of graduates in almost every field consider their work unrelated to their training. Social science majors think their jobs are least related to their disciplines; most related are those in the professional areas—engineering, education, and business.

Do those who say they are in unrelated jobs think they have been pushed into these jobs because of unavailable related jobs, or do they think they have been pulled into these positions because they are more desirable—better pay, greater opportunity for advancement, and so on? Apparently, many B.A.-level scientists of both sexes holding jobs unrelated to their college majors have been pushed out of their fields, while B.A. recipients in other fields have left to take advantage of better opportunities.

In the study of 1961 and 1966 freshman cohorts followed up in 1971, advanced-degree graduates (in the 1961 cohort) are more likely than B.A. graduates to be working in the field for which they trained: 85 percent compared with 64 percent for men; 87 percent compared with 71 percent for women (Bisconti and Gomberg 1975a). Of the B.A.'s in both cohorts, only a small proportion of liberal arts majors find employment in occupations usually classified as related to their field. However, many liberal arts majors in the 1961 cohort think they are working in a related job, even though they have occupational titles not generally considered related.

Contrary to widespread belief, then, the 1961–66 freshman study found that large numbers of arts and humanities and social science majors think they are using their college training in their work. Furthermore, the relationship between major field and employment is more important in determining job satisfaction for arts and humanities, social sciences, and biological sciences majors than for majors in chemistry and engineering (Bisconti and Gomberg 1975a). This area—the relationship between college training and employment —is the focus of the present study.

CHAPTER

3

THE MEANING OF
AN EDUCATION-RELATED JOB

The movement toward career education has expanded the ways in which education is viewed as useful for the world of work. Career education is more than vocational/technical education: Going beyond training for a single job or occupation, career education considers how education affects the total of one's life work. The development of life work, representing many choices throughout a lifetime, is influenced by many factors in addition to technical skills (NIE 1974). Hence, education may achieve career-education goals if it helps people not only develop work-related competencies but also realistic decisions about the educational requirements for attaining career goals. Career-education goals for society are met if education improves economic production and social service through better matching individual talents and societal needs and increasing awareness of how the economy functions and the importance of human resources (NIE 1974).

Some have argued that career education is not synonymous with education in general. Career education, which focuses on the interface between the individual and the economic sector, is primarily concerned with education as it relates to career development. More broadly, education is concerned with the development of critical thinking and the love of learning, transmission of diverse cultural heritages, and full participation of individuals in their society (NIE 1974). Of course, this differentiation between career and general education begs the question of whether the development of critical thinking and so on is important in achieving goals said to be career-education oriented.

One consequence of this career-education movement is the evaluation of education in terms of the extent to which it is used in the world of work. A problem of interpretation arises when an employer hires someone with educational attainment or skills above the minimum required and then adjusts the job to take advantage of the greater skills. An example is the secretary. Clearly, most employers would agree that a high school education is the minimum requirement for a secretary. However, today, many secretaries have advanced degrees. Some draw the conclusion that secretaries are underemployed; that is, their education is not suited to their careers. However, as they possess more education and greater skills, secretaries may be asked to perform tasks that clearly could not be handled by those possessing only minimal requirements. Jobs probably are modified to utilize the skills of those who hold them.

What aspects of college training are career related from the viewpoint of those who have received the training? Which definitions of career education put forth by federal officials and others are valid?

The most direct way to decide whether education is related to careers is to determine the extent to which the substance of college courses is used on the job. However, many other traits that can be acquired in college contribute to job success: clear thinking, ability to learn, appreciation of learning, leadership, ability to develop life goals, and others. The little empirical evidence that has been available on the education-work relationship has been limited to responses to such questions as, "Are you working in a job which is related to your major?" What does this mean to people? What is a related job? This study asked a wide variety of questions intended to extract data on the use of education in work, to understand the various dimensions of work, and to explain what people mean when they say their job is related to their major. Their answers tell us about respondents' perceptions of their general college experience and of what they got out of college which was directly used in work. To what extent can individual differences in perceptions of the relationship of education to careers be explained by perceptions of how specific aspects of college directly apply on the job? To what extent can they be explained by perceptions of how college affects individuals in ways they do not directly impact on career success?

To see whether people are matched to their jobs, one can compare the educational requirements for particular jobs with the educational attainment of individuals in these jobs. The *Occupational Outlook Handbook* (BLS 1974) describes jobs in the United States and specifies their minimum standards. Although occasionally the work is explained, little attempt is made to see that minimum educational requirements are consistent with the job. Those holding the jobs are not questioned.

Another approach to determining the match between education and jobs looks at the names of majors and of jobs and asks who falls into a job category with the same name as the major. For example, if an accounting major is working as an accountant, he is automatically assumed to be working in a related or matched job. However, this study found that only 80 percent of business administration majors working as accountants think they are closely related jobs; 70 percent in administration and 72 percent who are business owners think they are in related jobs. The literal definition of relationship does not always apply.

Table 3.1 shows perceptions of the relationship of job to college major by specific occupations. In which occupations are people most likely to consider their jobs related to their major? Seventy-nine percent of health professionals, 77 percent of accountants, 84 percent in allied health jobs, 84 percent of natural scientists, and 82 percent of teachers think their jobs are closely related to their major. Almost all these occupations require career-specific training except, possibly, teachers. Apparently, arts and humanities preparation is considered career specific for teachers of humanities subjects.

In what occupations are people least likely to consider their jobs related to their major? Fifty-two percent of administrative assistants and 50 percent of computer programmers think their jobs are not related to their major. Many in skilled, semiskilled, business-related, and transportation-related jobs feel, too, that their jobs are not related to their college training. In many of these areas, the number of respondents was small. Nevertheless, large proportions of people in secretarial fields (74 percent), sales (45 percent), military (47 percent), business owners (34 percent), buyers (37 percent), and counselors (39 percent) think they are in unrelated jobs.

A small percentage of those in jobs not closely related to their major appear to be holding those jobs involuntarily (Table 3.1). Respondents were asked why they were not in related jobs. Those who indicated the following responses were assumed to hold their job voluntarily: "never planned to take a closely related job," "prefer line of work not closely related," "tried closely related employment but did not like it," "first job was unrelated to major and I became interested in this type of work," "joined family business or firm," "found a better paying job," "found a job that offers a better chance for career advancement," "no longer in closely related job due to promotion." Those who gave the following responses were assumed to hold their job involuntarily: "wanted part-time work, flexible hours," "wanted to work at home," "am on temporary assignment" (Vista, Peace Corps, USIA, Foreign Service, missionary work, and so forth), "jobs related to major are not available where I live and I do not want to move," "am in the military," "could not get a closely related job but would prefer one," "limited in job selection by situation of spouse, family responsibilities," "very few jobs are related to my major," "employment opportunities are scarce for people in jobs related to my major."

To jump ahead and present evidence that will be elaborated upon later, it should be noted that job satisfaction is much lower for those holding their unrelated job involuntarily, whereas those voluntarily in unrelated jobs are almost as satisfied as those in related jobs.

TABLE 3.1

Occupation, by Relation of Job to College Major (in percentages)

Occupation	N	Relation of Job to Major			Voluntarily Related		Involuntarily Related	
		Closely	Somewhat	Not	Somewhat	Not	Somewhat	Not
Accountant	204	77	14	9	11	8	3	0
Middle administrator	228	18	30	52	24	41	6	11
Business administrator	463	39	33	28	31	26	3	2
Education administrator	41	37	39	24	34	22	5	2
Government administrator	138	31	39	30	36	27	4	3
Allied health worker	184	84	9	6	5	5	4	2
Architect	36	75	17	8	14	6	3	3
Business owner	175	35	31	34	29	33	2	2
Buyer	38	34	29	37	29	29	0	8
Clergy	17	65	18	18	6	18	12	0
Computer programmer	74	14	36	50	32	45	4	5
Computer scientist	150	13	49	39	45	39	3	0
Conservationist	23	61	30	9	22	9	9	0
Communication specialist	119	37	36	27	29	24	7	3
Counselor	33	21	39	39	27	30	12	9
Artist	31	55	19	26	16	19	3	6
Engineer	293	64	32	4	27	3	5	0
Farmer	56	36	34	30	30	29	4	2

(continued)

45

(Table 3.1 continued)

Occupation	N	Relation of Job to Major			Voluntarily Related		Involuntarily Related	
		Closely	Somewhat	Not	Somewhat	Not	Somewhat	Not
Foreign service worker	3	33	67	0	33	0	33	0
Health professional	28	79	14	7	7	7	7	0
Librarian	28	14	57	29	39	18	18	11
Law enforcement officer	28	11	36	54	36	39	0	14
Mathematician	17	47	29	24	18	12	12	12
Military person	111	12	41	47	22	32	19	14
Salesperson	322	24	30	45	28	41	2	4
Natural scientist	88	84	11	4	7	4	4	0
Social scientist	6	17	83	0	67	0	17	0
Secretary	145	12	14	74	8	40	7	34
Social welfare worker	142	47	29	24	18	15	11	9
Teacher	1,383	82	12	6	8	4	4	2
Professor	48	75	17	8	8	6	8	2
Technician	48	42	31	27	17	19	15	8
Transportation worker	17	6	18	77	18	59	0	18
Skilled worker	25	4	28	68	20	56	8	12
Semiskilled worker	17	6	12	82	6	47	6	35
Unskilled worker	12	0	0	100	0	25	0	75
Other	503	29	29	42	24	36	6	6

Table 3.2 provides the degree of satisfaction of those in jobs not closely related to their major, according to the reasons their job is not closely related. Of those indicating they are voluntarily not in closely related jobs, between 52 percent and 72 percent are very satisfied. Job satisfaction varies greatly depending upon the reason for being in an unrelated job involuntarily. Of those who are involuntarily holding jobs not closely related, between 15 percent and 71 percent are very satisfied, with most reasons given by groups in which less than 57 percent are very satisfied. If those in the military are left out, the range becomes 15 percent to 56 percent very satisfied.

TABLE 3.2

Satisfaction, by Reason Job Is Not Closely Related to Major
(in percentages)

Reason	N Giving Reason	Very Satisfied
Voluntary		
Never planned to take a closely related job	548	58
Prefer line of work not closely related	615	58
Tried closely related employment, but did not like	445	53
First job was unrelated and I became interested in this type of work	755	52
Joined family business	177	72
Found better-paying job	509	56
Found job that offers better chance for career advancement	707	65
No longer in closely related job due to promotion	126	56
Involuntary		
Wanted part-time work, flexible hours	111	39
Wanted to work at home	104	56
Am on a temporary assignment	24	38
Jobs related to major are not available where I live and I do not want to move	335	38
Am in the military	124	71
Could not get a closely related job, but would prefer one	277	15
Limited in job selection by situation of spouse, family responsibilities	291	30
Very few jobs are related to my major	566	43
Employment opportunities are scarce for people in jobs related to my major	605	38

TIME FRAME FOR CAREER SELECTION

It is unlikely that people will prepare for some particular occupations in college. Some jobs require less than a baccalaureate education. Once again, if these job holders have more than the minimum education necessary, the jobs may be modified. Certain jobs may require knowledge and skills that build upon a college education but are not often taught in college; in this case, actual tasks might be learned in another setting. Careers are often selected after college or at least after the time when college education can be tailored to later job plans. Certain jobs require skills that can only be picked up on the job. Table 3.3 shows when individuals in particular occupations decided on their type of work. The occupations are those for which there were more than 100 respondents. Although this selection might imply that only occupations with college training as a minimum requirement are included, in almost all occupations many individuals in society as a whole have less than a college degree.

For allied health, engineering, and teaching, over 40 percent of job holders selected their occupation before entering college. Since these jobs require specific curricula, individuals have to decide on the occupation before college or soon thereafter. Accounting is another occupation that should be selected early; in this case, a majority selected it either before or during college. Over

TABLE 3.3

Occupation, by Time of Selection (in percentages)

Occupation	N*	Before College	During College	At Graduation Time	Within 5 Years After	More Recently
Accountant	205	19	40	14	20	6
Administrator (middle, business, government)	833	7	12	22	44	15
Allied health worker	186	54	23	6	14	4
Business owner	175	9	16	11	37	27
Computer programmer and scientist	227	2	10	26	56	6
Communications specialist	118	19	20	14	36	11
Engineer	293	47	20	11	17	6
Military person	110	19	38	19	20	4
Salesperson	223	5	6	16	45	28
Secretary	145	9	8	21	40	22
Social welfare worker	144	15	28	17	34	6
Teacher	1,384	45	36	9	9	1
Total	4,043	26	24	15	28	10

*Only occupations with an N ≥ 100 are reported here.

half of those in the military selected their occupation before or during college. Experience with military-related programs, such as ROTC, while in college may be a major factor in this career choice.

Most other occupations are selected after graduation but within five years thereafter. These occupations fall into two groups: those into which individuals move because they are promoted or because they make a conscious decision to better themselves, and those selected because they are preferred to so-called more related jobs. Into the first group fall such occupations as administration, where individuals working in more education-related areas, such as laboratories or production or teaching or research, take on more administrative responsibility until their prime activity changes from substantive to administrative. Similarly, individuals who begin as programmers and learn about macrocomputer systems might decide to become computer scientists after several years of lower-level jobs. Business owners, most of whom assume that position within five years after graduation, probably spent the time between graduation and ownership accumulating enough capital to afford their own business. In communications, new entrants take rather menial jobs to prepare for what is generally agreed upon as professional work within the industry. It is probably a number of years after graduation before individuals in communications view themselves as specialists, having moved up from office boy at a television station, for instance.

Some people, those involuntarily in unrelated jobs, probably ended up in their jobs by default; that is, because other opportunities more related to college training were unavailable. Except for specialized cases, most sales people, secretaries, and perhaps even social welfare workers probably aspire to jobs more directly related to their college training. They probably accepted their jobs after finding that the first few years beyond college did not lead to satisfactory jobs in college-related areas.

Table 3.4 indicates how beneficial college education is in providing knowledge and skills useful in the current job. Workers in certain occupations, such as accountancy, allied health, engineering, and education, are still most likely to think their college education is very useful after eight years of work. These are fields that require college-specific knowledge.

In a sense, two factors are at work. On the one hand, occupations that require specific college training must be selected before embarking on college. On the other hand, certain jobs that do not require specific college training can be held either by those who are unable to find jobs that use their college training or by individuals who were unable to select a curriculum to prepare themselves for a specific job. Certain jobs can be performed equally well, with or without a college education, even if the general competencies required to complete college are also required for the job.

College education has prepared few people for the following specific tasks performed by large numbers of college graduates: administration, manage-

TABLE 3.4

Occupation, by Usefulness of Education in Providing Knowledge and Skills (in percentages)

Occupation	Very Useful	Somewhat Useful	Not at All Useful
Accountant	62	36	2
Office worker	17	60	23
Administrator (business executive, and so forth)	25	62	13
Sales person	16	64	20
Mathematician and scientist	28	54	18
Allied health worker	82	16	2
Engineer	56	42	2
Educator	67	31	2
Social worker, counselor	43	52	6
Other professional	34	53	13
Other nonprofessional	14	60	26

Note: All miscellaneous occupations classified as other were further categorized as professional or not on the basis of responses to the item "I am working at a professional level."

ment, counseling, production, quality control, program planning, or budgeting (Bisconti and Solmon 1976). These positions are not low-level functions, even though they are most often learned on the job. A college education may greatly facilitate learning higher-level skills, even if these skills must be learned after the worker is in the job.

Table 3.5 shows how, in addition to college education, workers in different occupations acquire job skills. Although by far the most prevalent way is on-the-job training, much of this learning is probably incidental, that is, obtained as workers become experienced. However, in many occupations workers pick up additional skills in formal training programs either at the company (for example, sales people) or outside (for example, mathematicians or scientists). Few people indicate that no additional training is required beyond college.

Considering that a large number of high-level skills require experiential learning, should colleges prepare people to perform these high-level functions? College should provide the foundation on which people can build a solid career, while leaving to employers the responsibility to develop specific job competencies. Given changing career plans, job requirements, and employer needs, over-specific vocational-like training in many areas is probably not beneficial.

TABLE 3.5

Occupation, by Method Job Skills Are Acquired
(in percentages)

Occupation	On-the-Job Training	Picked It Up Myself	Formal Training (at the company or outside institution)	No Training Required
Accountant	93	45	62	1
Office worker	84	59	46	4
Administrator	87	64	65	1
Sales	90	57	79	0
Mathematician and scientist	90	52	88	1
Allied health worker	83	34	56	1
Engineer	88	61	58	2
Educator	72	66	30	4
Social worker and counselor	81	68	63	5
Other professional	84	58	63	2
Other nonprofessional	80	58	50	4

JOB LEVEL

Relationship may have several dimensions. Clearly, one is task orientation. If an individual is trained as a chemistry major and works with test tubes in a laboratory, his tasks are related to his college study. However, if the tasks involve cleaning test tubes as a lab assistant or filling them as a lab technician, a chemistry major may say he is not using his education in his job.

We hypothesized that another important dimension might be job level, particularly as it relates to expectations acquired in college. If this chemistry major is conducting lab experiments, the level of his job indicates he is working in his field, that is, at a related job. Individuals with adequate job status who make progress in their careers, use their skills, work at a professional level, and make sufficient income are likely to believe they are using their education. Moreover, people who work with colleagues and supervise people trained in the same field are likely to think they are using their education. Studying the correlation between the substance of college courses and the tasks college graduates perform is not the only route to defining the relationship of education and work. Job level as well as job content must be considered.

To see whether the level of particular jobs affects workers' perceptions of relationship between education and occupation, regressions were run for individuals within those occupations for which there were sufficient respondents.

These regressions attempted to determine whether variables indicating the job level were significant in explaining the relationship variable. The relationship variable was a response to the question, "How closely related is your job to your undergraduate major field?"*

The independent or explanatory variables indicating job level reflected whether individuals felt they had sufficient job status, they were making satisfactory career progress, their skills were fully utilized on the job, and they were working at a professional level. An income variable was included because one would expect income to be a good indicator of job level. It is striking that, within occupations, little of the individual difference in relationship was explained by the five variables indicating job level. Other variables accounted for a much higher proportion of variance (R^2).

In only one occupation—communications specialists (reporter, writer, television advertising, public relations)—is sufficient job status a predictor of relationship, and the sign of the job-status variable was negative. Those not using their training, perhaps because they have developed skills beyond those acquired in college, think they have sufficient job status. Apparently, utilization of skills, working at a professional level, and income are somewhat more powerful predictors of relationship. However, in cases where these variables are significant, the explanatory power of the model is still low (Table 3.6).

Since the study explains many individual differences in perceptions of how related education is to jobs by a different set of variables, the distinction between perceptions of relationship that depend on level of job and those which depend on the work done on the job is probably not strong.

Table 3.7 provides the percentage of men and women in each occupational field which responded to the variables hypothesized as indicating job level within an occupation. Although variation is substantial, depending on the specific aspect of job level, it appears that generally women think they have slightly lower-level jobs within occupations except on skills fully used. For some occupations, the respondents of a particular sex are too few to generalize. The most notable sex difference is in income, where 61 percent of women but under 10 percent of men earn below $10,000. This difference might result because more women than men worked in the past when salaries were lower but are not working now.

In Table 3.8, which provides data on income by time when last worked, only 8 percent of men and 36 percent of women currently working fall into the bottom third of the income distribution, whereas those who are not currently working but have worked fall into the bottom third much more frequently (42

---

*The responses were coded so that "closely related" received a three, "somewhat related" a two, and "not related" a one.

TABLE 3.6

Predicting Relationship Using Job Level Variables, by Occupation (beta weights)

Job Level Variable	Administration (Middle, Business, Government)	Allied Health	Computer Science and Programming	Communications Specialist	Engineering	Sales	Secretary	Social Welfare	Teaching
Sufficient job status or prestige	.013	.039	-.125	-.256*	.021	-.089	.086	-.133	.010
Satisfied with career progress to date	-.045	.023	.000	.069	.008	.114	.092	.137	.066*
Skills are fully utilized in my job	.152*	-.058	.144*	-.018	.155*	.032	.136	.294*	.130*
Am working at a professional level	.093*	.337*	-.129	.267*	-.023	-.026	.022	-.011	.000
Income	.136*	.156*	.156*	-.011	.141*	.008	.103	-.072	-.026
R^2	.062	.114	.054	.124	.052	.015	.096	.107	.028
N	809	176	221	115	285	315	116	134	1,328

*Significant at the .05 level.

TABLE 3.7

Occupation, by Occupational Level and Sex (in percentages)

Occupation	N Men	N Women	Sufficient Status Men	Sufficient Status Women	Career Progress Men	Career Progress Women	Skills Fully Used Men	Skills Fully Used Women	Professional Level Men	Professional Level Women	Income Men Low	Income Men Mid	Income Men High	Income Women Low	Income Women Mid	Income Women High
Accountant	181	17	68	76	64	71	40	29	77	65	3	40	57	37	53	11
Middle administrator	123	97	53	47	54	38	15	11	46	38	6	65	29	56	42	2
Business administrator	425	39	84	82	83	80	36	38	65	80	1	28	70	18	41	41
Education administrator	31	11	74	54	55	36	29	64	71	100	10	63	27	64	18	18
Government administrator	106	32	70	78	67	84	34	44	80	97	3	51	46	9	67	24
Allied health	43	140	65	61	67	53	35	45	81	81	7	44	49	53	46	1
Architect	32	4	72	50	69	25	44	50	88	50	9	66	25	25	75	0
Business owner	158	17	77	88	69	47	38	18	43	6	9	26	66	53	35	12
Buyer	28	11	68	82	46	91	7	18	39	46	7	61	32	18	82	0
Clergy	12	5	83	40	58	60	58	60	75	60	67	33	0	80	20	0
Computer programmer	36	38	44	50	44	68	25	16	64	53	3	73	24	22	70	8
Computer science	113	38	64	76	55	71	23	34	79	82	0	37	63	10	40	50
Conservationist	20	3	80	33	75	33	35	33	80	67	10	70	20	100	0	0
Communications specialist	60	57	77	65	68	53	33	28	87	67	5	61	34	37	51	12
Counselor	18	15	61	80	61	33	11	20	83	53	17	78	6	56	44	0
Artist	17	14	35	64	29	57	41	71	82	71	71	29	0	69	31	0
Engineer	286	5	64	60	60	40	30	20	76	80	1	41	58	25	50	25
Farmer	53	5	79	40	58	40	42	0	28	0	34	50	16	100	0	0

54

Foreign service	2	1	100	0	50	0	100	0	100	0	0	100	0	100	0	0
Health professional	11	17	73	65	82	59	46	47	100	88	0	46	54	47	53	0
Librarian	1	26	0	54	0	58	0	27	0	58	100	0	0	70	30	0
Law enforcement officer	26	1	89	100	81	100	23	0	69	100	0	35	65	0	50	50
Mathematician	11	6	82	50	82	50	18	17	54	50	9	36	54	33	50	17
Military person	109	3	88	100	85	100	38	0	82	100	1	34	65	33	67	0
Salesperson	288	31	67	64	58	55	22	16	63	55	6	34	60	47	38	16
Natural scientist	49	38	61	58	53	55	33	40	76	60	8	67	24	49	46	5
Social scientist	3	3	67	100	67	67	0	33	67	67	0	33	67	100	0	0
Secretary	10	108	40	30	40	19	30	6	20	6	70	20	10	89	11	0
Social welfare worker	21	118	57	58	38	54	24	24	81	77	32	68	0	59	40	2
Teacher	309	1,050	56	64	57	62	35	42	76	75	19	78	3	69	31	0
Professor	18	28	67	71	61	57	61	50	83	86	20	80	0	59	33	7
Technician	31	15	39	47	42	27	10	47	39	53	39	54	6	87	13	0
Transportation worker	13	2	69	50	38	0	15	0	38	0	20	67	13	50	50	0
Skilled worker	20	1	50	0	40	0	5	0	0	0	30	56	13	100	0	0
Semiskilled worker	10	3	20	33	30	0	0	0	0	0	50	50	0	100	0	0
Unskilled worker	7	0	43	—*	29	—	0	—	0	—	77	15	8	—	—	—
Other	311	183	69	61	61	55	26	31	69	62	12	42	47	56	32	11
Total	5,174		68	61	64	57	31	35	68	67	9	46	45	61	35	4

*No women fall into unskilled category.

TABLE 3.8

Income Level, by Work Period and Sex (in percentages)

Income	Men					Women				
	Currently Full-time	Worked in Past, Not Now				Currently Full-time	Worked in Past, Not Now			
		Total	Within Last 3 Months	4–12 Months Ago	Over 1 Year Ago		Total	Within Last 3 Months	4–12 Months Ago	Over 1 Year Ago
Low ($0–9,999)	8	42	31	42	54	36	81	67	70	83
Middle ($10,000–16,999)	46	44	55	39	38	55	18	29	28	16
High ($17,000 and over)	46	14	14	18	8	7	1	5	2	1
N	2,995	88	—	—	—	1,021	1,302	—	—	—

percent of men and 81 percent of women). The further into the past men and women held their last job, the more likely they are to be in the lowest income group.

For both sexes, the occupations of middle-level administrator, buyer, computer programmer, counselor, farmer, foreign service worker, librarian, salesperson, social scientist, secretary, social welfare worker, technician, transportation worker, and the various categories of manual workers include the most individuals holding low-level jobs (indicated by the lower percentages in Table 3.7). In many of these occupations, women appear more frequently than they do in other occupations. In such occupations as secretary or salesperson, many people performing these jobs see that they are not working at a professional level or making full use of their skills. However, those with advanced education may work better because of their background. Secretaries with more education might, indeed, perform different functions than secretaries with little education. However, certain occupational categories, such as secretary, by their nature are perceived as low level, regardless of the tasks performed.

USEFULNESS OF EDUCATION IN WORK

What aspects of the college experience are used on the job, and what job characteristics lead individuals to perceive that their jobs are closely related to their college major? The survey questionnaire (Appendix A) asked many questions pertaining to the interface between education and work. Some deal with the same factor in slightly different ways.

For example, as well as asking, "How closely related is your job to your undergraduate major field?" the questionnaire also asked, "How frequently do you use each of several aspects of college education in your current job?" One subquestion of this was concerned with how frequently one uses the course content of the undergraduate major. Hence, it was possible to differentiate between use of course content and value in job of pursuing a major that provides general knowledge, ability to learn, and similar attributes that do not explicitly involve the course content.

Table 3.9 summarizes ratings of usefulness of college education for respondents' current jobs. The largest proportion of individuals indicated usefulness in terms of "increasing general knowledge" and "increasing chances of finding a good job." Sixty percent indicated that the bachelor's degree was a factor in being hired by the current employer.

In addition to the aspects of relationship apparent from the questionnaire, certain responses were used to construct other "relationship" variables. For example, respondents recommended courses that would be most useful for someone preparing for a job like theirs. Table 3.10 shows the study areas most

TABLE 3.9

Ratings of Usefulness of College Education for Job (in percentages)

Educational Benefit	Usefulness for Job		
	Very	Somewhat	Not at All
It increased my general knowledge	73	27	*
It increased my chances of finding a good job	69	27	5
My bachelor's degree was a factor in my being hired by my current employer	60	21	19
It increased my ability to think clearly	43	53	4
It taught me a skill that enabled me to get my first job	42	29	29
It gave me knowledge and skills that I use in my current job	38	50	12
It increased my leadership ability	22	58	20
It helped me choose my life goals	21	49	29
The contacts I made in college with professors or friends helped me get my current job	5	11	84

*Indicates less than half of 1 percent.

TABLE 3.10

Study Areas Recommended for Own Job by Workers in All Occupations

Study Area	Percentage of All Workers Recommending
Business administration	45
English	32
Psychology	31
Economics	28
Accounting	27
Mathematics	23
Social sciences	18
Education	17
Engineering	17
Other business	15
Arts and humanities	14
Other social sciences	11
Biological sciences	11
Chemistry	10
History	9
Physics	8
Languages	8

recommended overall, regardless of particular job: The most frequently recommended area is business administration, since many workers probably believe that business-related skills are useful on the job. However, the second most frequently recommended area is English, a subject not generally viewed as vocational. Clearly, it is the grammar, writing, and reading abilities most people are recommending, rather than knowledge of Shakespearean plots. Psychology is the third most frequently recommended study area, probably because workers believe getting along with people rather than knowing how to conduct experiments, is a useful skill for work.

In reconstructing one of the relationship variables, responses to the question of what courses are recommended for one's job were recoded according to whether an individual recommended courses in his own major for the job he currently held. If an individual indicated that he was working at a job closely related to his major or that he was using the content of his major courses but he did not recommend that major as preparation, this response might be significant in our understanding of the education-job relationship.

In reconstructing a second relationship variable, responses to a list of work activities were used which indicated not only those that the respondents were currently performing, but also those for which their college education prepared them. For each individual, tallies were made of the activities for which they were prepared but which they were not currently using. This variable (called "useless") was developed to test the hypothesis that even if one uses certain aspects of college training, if that training provides additional skills not used, the individual will perceive that he is not making use of his college education.

A third variable looked at the activities an individual was performing and calculated a proportion of those for which his college education trained him. The share of activities was hypothesized to be another dimension of how related a job is to the college experience.

VARIABLES TO EXPLAIN RELATIONSHIP

In the first attempt to determine the relationship between education and job, the forward (stepwise) multiple regression method of selecting independent variables from among the complete list available was used. In this method, the independent variable that explains the greatest amount of variance in the dependent variable enters first; the variable that explains the greatest amount of variance in conjunction with the first enters second, and so on. This list comprised not only variables directly retrievable from the questionnaire but also those constructed from other questionnaire responses. The dependent variable in these analyses was the question, "How closely related is your job to your undergraduate major field?"*

Eight independent variables were chosen from the complete list and entered into the regressions presented here. Among them were variables indicating the degree to which the respondent uses the content of his major courses on the job; whether the respondent worked with colleagues who are trained in this field; whether he recommended his major to someone preparing for his job; and whether he indicated that his college education provided him with knowledge useful in his current job. The variable "useless" indicated the number of activities for which college trained an individual but which he is not using on his current job. Other variables indicated the individual's use of the content of other (nonmajor) undergraduate courses in his job, whether the respondent supervised people trained in his field, and whether college training gave one the ability to think clearly. Table B.1 describes why these eight variables were chosen.

---

*Among the statistical problems with this approach was the excessive multicolinearity among the independent variables. Since this regression allowed any and all possible explanatory variables to enter, a reduced number of variables were selected to define relationship.

The study hypothesized that an individual would be more likely to indicate the relationship between his education and job if he was working with colleagues or supervising people trained in his field. Moreover, the ability to think clearly in and of itself and as a proxy for some omitted variables would be perceived by some as valuable on the job, even though this characteristic is usually thought to have broader impacts than merely usefulness in work.

Table B.2 presents simple correlation between the relationship-defining variables and the extent to which one's job is closely related to one's major field. Table B.3 presents intercorrelations of the relationship variables. Even though all variables in these tables are not included in the regressions described in this chapter, the total possible set of relationships is displayed in Tables B.2 and B.3.

DEFINING AN EDUCATION-RELATED JOB

Approximately 60 percent of individual variance was explained in responses to the question "How closely related is your job to your undergraduate major field?" by the eight variables: frequency of use of major courses, frequency of use of other undergraduate courses, the usefulness of college education in increasing ability to think clearly, the usefulness of college education in providing knowledge and skills used in current job, whether the respondent supervised people trained in his field, whether most of his colleagues were trained in his field, whether he recommended his major for someone else preparing for a job like his, and the number of activities for which his college education prepared him but which he is not performing in his job.

The greater the frequency of use of undergraduate major courses, the more likely the respondent to view his job as closely related to his field. This result, obvious as it is, confirms that use of course content is the most powerful predictor of perceptions of the relationship between college major and job. One might expect that other aspects of the college experience were more useful, and these might be perceived as contributing more to the relationships of education to work. After controlling for the fact that individuals use or do not use the content of their major courses, there are other highly significant predictors of the perception that college major is related to one's current job. Table 3.11 summarizes regressions to explain individual differences in the extent to which college major is related to one's job.

Table 3.12 provides detail on how frequently individuals with different majors indicate they use their course content. Those in education use their major most frequently, followed by those in business, natural sciences, and engineering. Minor courses are used most frequently by education majors (who may teach their minor).

TABLE 3.11

Independent Variables Defining Relationship Subjectively, by Sex
(betas in final step)

Variable	Total	Men	Women
Use content of major courses	.607	.573	.631
Colleagues trained in my field	.155	.114	.193
Recommend major as preparation for job	.110	.131	.083
College taught knowledge and skills used in current job	.114	.139	.094
Number of work activities college prepared but not using	−.066	−.057	−.073
Use content of other undergraduate courses	−.062	−.091	−.025[*]
College increased ability to think clearly	−.048	−.036	−.067
Supervise people in my field	.040	.068	.014[*]
R^2	.602	.580	.631

[*] Not significant at the .05 level. All the other variables are significant at the .05 level.

Table 3.13 shows which majors in which occupations use their major course content frequently or almost aways. Administrators, educators, and "other" professionals use the content frequently or almost always regardless of major. In other fields, specific majors are frequently used.

After controlling for the extent to which the content is used on the job (see Table 3.11), individuals who recommend their major for people preparing for a job like theirs are more likely to feel their job is closely related. A number of people use their major but feel that other preparations are more appropriate for a job like theirs. Those who recommend their own major as preparation are even more likely to feel their jobs are closely related. After controlling for these two variables, an indication that college education provides knowledge useful in the current job added to the power of the regression. This response probably represents knowledge, in addition to specific major course content, useful on the job, including that from other courses, as well as experience in problem solving, learning how to learn, time management, and the like.

The meaning of these variables comes into sharper focus in considering three additional significant explanatory variables that enter the equation with negative signs. The greater the extent to which other (nonmajor) courses are used on the job, the less likely the respondent to indicate that his undergraduate major is closely related to his job.

TABLE 3.12

Use of Course Content in Work, by Major
(in percentages)

Course	Almost Always/ Frequently	Sometimes	Rarely	Never
English				
Major	44	23	21	12
Minor	27	32	25	17
Other	21	42	26	12
Arts and humanities (other)				
Major	35	19	23	22
Minor	29	28	23	21
Other	25	45	23	8
Economics				
Major	37	36	20	8
Minor	30	34	21	14
Other	21	50	23	6
Social sciences				
Major	24	26	30	21
Minor	25	28	25	21
Other	21	48	23	9
Natural sciences				
Major	51	19	18	12
Minor	33	33	20	14
Other	22	50	24	4
Mathematics				
Major	37	33	23	7
Minor	20	29	28	3
Other	18	47	29	6
Business				
Major	55	31	11	2
Minor	27	37	25	11
Other	17	49	29	5
Education				
Major	61	23	10	6
Minor	40	29	18	14
Other	30	50	15	5
Engineering				
Major	49	28	20	3
Minor	22	44	21	13
Other	18	48	29	5

TABLE 3.13

Majors Using Major Course Content Almost Always or Frequently, by Occupation (in percentages)

Major	Accountant	Office Worker	Administrator	Sales	Mathematics and Sciences	Allied Health	Engineer	Educator	Other Professional	Other Nonprofessional
English	—	—	47	—	—	—	—	73	34	23
Arts and humanities (other)	—	—	18	—	—	—	—	70	33	22
Economics	—	9	32	40	—	—	—	—	39	30
Social sciences	—	—	19	21	—	—	—	53	20	—
Natural sciences	—	—	31	—	59	88	—	74	48	—
Mathematics	—	—	14	—	19	—	—	75	—	—
Business	84	—	60	39	—	—	—	—	40	—
Education	—	—	—	—	—	—	—	75	—	—
Engineering	—	—	26	—	—	—	63	—	—	—

Note: Percents shown for occupations reported by 10 percent or more of respondents in each major field—for example, 10 percent or more of English majors reported being administrators, and, therefore, the table shows the percent of English majors employed as administrators who use the content of their major "almost always or frequently."

This negative coefficient represents the partial correlation between relationship and degree of use of nonmajor courses, holding constant such factors as the extent of use of major courses and perceptions of the degree to which college provided knowledge and skills useful in the job. For a given degree of use of major courses and perception of contribution by college of useful skills, the more nonmajor courses used, the less likely the respondent to view his job as related to his major. Use of nonmajor courses is viewed as an alternative to relationship of job to major rather than as a reinforcer of that relationship. For a given degree of use of content of major and nonmajor courses, the greater the degree to which college education provides knowledge and skills useful in the current job, the greater the perceived relationship between job and major. The provision-of-knowledge variable reinforces the relationship perception. The relationship of job to major depends not only on use of major course content, but also on provision by college of a wider set of competencies. Given this, workers who hold jobs requiring use of nonmajor courses are less likely to perceive a link between job and major.

Similarly, the larger the number of activities for which college prepared an individual but which are not being performed on the current job, the less likely the individual to indicate that his college major is closely related to his current job. If an individual has been prepared for many activities, only some of which appear useful, the likelihood is greater that the college education appears unrelated. If one goal of college training is to provide education that will be perceived as related to later work, then it does not seem necessary to prepare an individual with a broad set of skills in addition to the skills and knowledge acquired from his concentration and from the more general college experience. Individuals prepared to do things they are not doing and those using knowledge acquired in nonmajor courses are less likely to perceive their jobs as related to their undergraduate major. Of course, the important underlying question is whether perceiving one's job as related to one's major is a meaningful goal. This investigation is meant to determine just that.

Those who indicate that their college education gave them the ability to think clearly are less likely to indicate that their job is closely related to college major. Possibly, those in unrelated jobs are attempting to rationalize the usefulness of their college experience by indicating that the training provides a generally useful skill, even if it is not directly related to current work.

The characteristics of co-workers, both peers and subordinates, are significant determinants of the perception of relationship of job to major. Individuals who supervise and work with people trained in the same field are more likely to indicate that their job is closely related to their major, even after controlling for all the above factors. If a worker is not significantly more likely to use his major or to feel that the job provides opportunities to use additional attributes from college, and if he is equally likely to use nonmajor courses and to be prepared for work he is not doing, the fact that he is working with or supervising people trained in his major gives him a feeling that his job and major are related.

Although all variables are highly significant for the total respondents, the four variables with the highest degree of significance (that is, the highest partial correlations with the dependent variable) are indications that the content of major courses is used frequently, that one is working with colleagues trained in the same field, that one's major is recommended for someone training for the same job, and that college education provides knowledge and skills useful in the job. Three of these deal directly with the positive contribution of the major courses and other noncourse experiences in college.

SEX DIFFERENCES IN PERCEPTIONS OF RELATIONSHIP

The same regression equation was estimated separately for men and women. Although the coefficients differed somewhat, the signs for both were always identical. In only two cases—an indication by women that they supervise people trained in their field and that they use the content of other courses— are the predictor variables not statistically significant. The first one is not surprising, given the low frequency of women in supervisory positions. Because there was a statistically significant difference (according to the Chow test, $F=5.96$) in the relationship for men and for women, the various explanatory variables had different weights in the male and female equations. A weight, or impact of a particular factor, is a function both of the mean value of a variable and the correlation between that variable and the dependent variable. In both cases, indication of the frequency of use of major courses has at least three times the weight of any other factor in explaining the dependent variable. However, for men, the next two most important factors are an indication that one recommends one's major for someone preparing for the job and an indication that knowledge obtained in college is useful on the current job. However, for women, after an indication of use of major courses, the next most powerful variable was an indication that the respondent works with colleagues trained in the same field. Perhaps women are more sensitive than men about interpersonal aspects of a job (in particular, the characteristics of colleagues) when they evaluate the relationship between their college major and their job. The three regressions explaining the relationship between college major and job appear in Table 3.11, which provides the beta weights. Table 3.14 demonstrates the derivation of weights to predict the relationship that considers both the B coefficient and the mean value of the variables in the cases of men, women, and total separately. Except for the variable indicating that college education provided the ability to think clearly, the mean values of all independent and dependent variables are significantly different for men and women.

TABLE 3.14

Derivation of Weights to Predict Relation of Job to Major Subjectively, by Sex

Variable	Total			Men			Women		
	B*	Mean	Weight	B*	Mean	Weight	B*	Mean	Weight
Use content of major courses	.39448	3.36	33.4	.38184	3.23	35.0	.39685	3.54	38.8
Colleagues trained in my field	.27328	1.33	9.1	.20997	1.27	7.6	.32400	1.41	12.6
Recommend major as preparation for job	.18471	1.60	7.4	.22045	1.62	10.1	.13916	1.57	6.0
College taught knowledge and skills used in current job	.14035	2.24	7.9	.17611	2.23	11.2	.11111	2.26	6.9
Number of work activities college prepared but not doing	-.03710	1.07	-1.0	-.02943	1.20	-1.0	-.04749	0.88	-1.2
Use content of other undergraduate courses	-.10410	1.40	-3.7	-.15348	1.37	-6.0	-.04147	1.45	-1.6
College increased my ability to think clearly	-.06950	2.39	-4.2	-.05176	2.40	-3.5	-.09857	2.39	-6.5
Supervise people in my field	.07610	1.25	2.4	.12025	1.31	4.5	.03156	1.15	1.0
Constant	.21543		5.4	.14041		4.0	.33608		9.3

*This is the raw coefficient, not the standardized beta weight.

EFFECTS OF ADDING OTHER VARIABLES

Table 3.15 extends the analysis by including, in addition to the independent variables in Table 3.11, a set of background and other variables that indicate characteristics of one's job level and career progress. The table shows to what degree the relationship-defining variables above retain their significance when other characteristics of the individual respondents, their college experience, and their jobs are included to explain the perception of the extent to which college major is related to job. Apparently, relationship-defining variables remain highly significant even after adding the background and other variables. In addition, the statistically significant difference between the male and the female equation persists (according to the Chow test, $F=3.45$).

In this larger regression, the first set of comments pertains to the variables that are not significant for either men or women. The study hypothesized that the higher the grade-point average in college, the more likely that one would perceive the undergraduate major as related to a job. College grade-point average is never significant in the regressions, perhaps because those with higher grade-point averages tend to vary in selecting jobs closely related to major. The study also hypothesized that the longer an individual stayed with the same employer, the less likely that he would be in a related job because he would probably have been promoted. This does not appear to be the case either, perhaps because those who stayed with the same employer for longer periods might still be working with or supervising colleagues trained in their field. These factors increase the probability of the perception of a closer job/major relationship, even though the respondent would no longer be using the specific major course content. Similarly, it was predicted that the number of years an individual has been employed full time will have a negative effect on the education-job relationship, but this prediction, too, never appears significant. Two variables indicating marital status were included to determine whether married men or single women, in particular, were more likely to pursue jobs related to their college major. It was hypothesized that married men would be more likely to take jobs that use their training, perhaps to avoid risky jobs when family responsibilities are evident. In other studies, single women are shown to have characteristics more like men. Hence, single women might be more likely to pursue careers that use their educational background. However, no marital-status variable appears significant in either the male or female regressions. The omitted dummy variable on marital status was "widowed, separated, divorced." The results indicate no significant differences between married and divorced or single and divorced. Finally, in determining whether an indication of satisfactory career progress would be related to the perception of relationship between education and job, the study indicated that those who feel they are making satisfactory progress are neither more nor less likely than others to perceive themselves as in closely related jobs.

TABLE 3.15

Relationship and Background Variables Defining Relationship Subjectively, by Sex (betas in final step)

Variable	Total	Men	Women
Relationship			
Use contant of major courses	.530*	.533*	.499*
Colleagues trained in my field	.103*	.088*	.103*
Recommend major as preparation for job	.108*	.127*	.079*
College taught knowledge and skills used in current job	.090*	.113*	.068*
Number of work activities college prepared but not doing	-.044*	-.044*	-.044*
Use content of other undergraduate courses	-.067*	-.088*	-.038*
College increased ability to think clearly	-.034*	-.027*	-.047*
Supervise people in my field	.056*	.071*	.033*
Background			
Sex	-.016	—	—
College grade-point average	-.004	-.008	.004
Selectivity of institution	-.037*	-.034*	-.036*
When chose my occupation	-.175*	-.136*	-.233*
Years with employer	-.003	-.002	-.019
Worked in past, not now	.024	-.002	.026
Years employed full time	-.002	.008	-.000
Number of graduate courses taken	-.003	-.012	.021
Business firm employer	.022	.057*	-.038*
Heavy industry employer	.058	.096*	-.017
Education employer	.091*	.080*	.058*
Government employer	.023*	.046*	-.006
Single	.007	.004	.014
Married	.007	.006	-.006
Level			
Design own work program	.017	.019	.010
Have policy responsibility	-.015	-.021	-.012
Sufficient job status	-.004	.010	-.023
Satisfied with career progress	-.010	-.016	-.004
Work at professional level	.024*	.005	.052*

*Significant at .05 level.

A number of the variables added in Table 3.15 do appear significantly related to perceptions of how closely related one's job is to one's major. Most significant is the variable indicating the time when an occupation is selected; the earlier the occupation is chosen (that is, before college), the more likely an individual to be in a job related to his major.

Four dummy variables indicated whether (value of two) or not (value of one) the respondent is employed in a particular sector (business, heavy industry, education, or government) to see whether that sector is related to the employee's perception of the relationship of his major to his job. One possible employment sector was omitted to act as a reference group for the comparison of all the other employment groups. The omitted sector—"other"—included human services, social welfare, health, and unknown sectors.

Respondents in the four sectors for which dummies were inserted are more likely than those in the "other" sector to perceive a strong relationship between major and job. Women in business firms—the only exception—are less likely to view their jobs as related to their major, probably because many are secretaries. Women in heavy industry and government are neither more nor less likely than those in the "other" sector to view their jobs as related, probably for the same reason. Both men and women in education are most likely to view their jobs as related. After men in education, men in heavy industry, and then business and government are most likely to view their jobs as related. Those in the latter two sectors are more likely to be administrators than to be working in the substantive area of their major.

Both men and women who attended more selective institutions (Astin 1971) are less likely to indicate that their jobs are closely related to their major, perhaps because those from more highly selective institutions are able to choose from a wider variety of jobs with more opportunities, even if they cannot use their specific major.

Only one level variable is significant. Women who think they are at a professional level are more likely to feel a relationship between their education and work. Possibly, women perceive themselves as at a professional level if they also think they are using their college training.

Table 3.16 summarizes some of the findings of Tables 3.11 and 3.15. It presents the R^2s after particular groups of variables were entered into the regression to explain relationship of major to job. The original eight relationship-defining variables explain 58 percent of the individual variance in the dependent variable for men and 63 percent for women. When adding the set of control variables, the R^2 increased to 60 percent for men and to 69 percent for women. The R^2 stayed approximately the same once the other variables were added. Table 3.16 confirms that the original eight variables thought to define relationship of major to work contribute almost all the explanatory power to the model. Even by adding personal, educational, and job characteristics, relationship is not predicted any more accurately. To explain approxi-

TABLE 3.16

R^2s after Each Step for Defining Relationship Subjectively,
by Total and Sex

Step	Total	Men	Women
Relationship	.60	.58	.63
Background	.63	.60	.69
Other (final)	.63	.60	.69

mately 60 percent of individual differences in the dependent variable is highly significant. The elements that lead to the prediction of a perception of relationship of major to job are readily apparent. They are, in general, three: the specific use of content of major courses on the job, other skills and knowledge acquired in college which are related neither to major nor to other course content, and the ability to work with or supervise individuals with similar training. The other variables that contribute to the definition of relationship are indeed significant but have less power.

DIFFERENCES BY MAJOR

Table 3.17 replicates Table 3.11, but it shows respondents divided by major. Individuals in this study indicated the field in which they took the most courses. That response was used as a proxy for major. In earlier studies, individuals sometimes were unable to respond to the specific question of major, since they had dual majors or were in general programs. In some cases, individuals may be considered in a particular major even though more courses were taken in other fields. This study is most concerned with individuals divided by the area in which they took the most courses.

Overall, about 60 percent of the individual variance in perceptions of relationship of college major to current job was explained by the eight proposed defining variables. Although 71 percent of the variance in responses of those majoring in arts and humanities other than English, and those majoring in the natural sciences can be explained, only 36 percent of the individual variance in responses of business majors can be explained. Those in other majors fall somewhere in between. Moreover, in each major not all eight variables appear significant. One variable is significant in every single field: the frequency of use of major course content on the job.

There are a number of reasons why particular variables would not be significantly related to the dependent variable for those in a particular major. On one hand, most people in a major might have responded identically to a question, even when all individuals felt that college contributed in the particular way

TABLE 3.17

Independent Variables Defining Relationship Subjectively, by Major
(betas in step after relationship variables enter)

Variable	English	Arts and Humanities	Economics	Social Sciences	Natural Sciences	Mathematics	Business	Education	Engineering
Use content of major courses	.597*	.720*	.630*	.564*	.620*	.534*	.448*	.459*	.395*
Colleagues trained in my field	.270*	.007*	.087	.144*	.109*	.134*	.064*	.299*	.168*
Recommend major as preparation for job	.099*	.071*	.039	.093*	.196*	.120*	.196*	.149*	.144*
College taught knowledge and skills used in current job	.102*	.104*	.069	.156*	.085*	.087	.035	.062*	.226*
Number of work activities college prepared but not doing	-.024	-.041	-.076	-.078*	-.079*	-.129*	-.078*	-.149*	-.116*
Use content of other undergraduate courses	-.042	-.043	-.026	-.006	-.035	-.041	-.076*	-.073*	-.114*
College increased my ability to think clearly	-.032	-.106*	-.010	-.051*	-.034	-.090*	-.018	-.041	-.062
Supervise people in my field	.014	.002	.064	.007	.016	-.046	.095*	-.023	.131*
R^2	.582	.706	.502	.563	.711	.493	.361	.556	.544
N	435	445	259	938	556	284	738	548	339

*Significant at .05 level.

implied by the question. For example, all English majors might have felt that their college training provided the ability to think clearly regardless of whether they felt their major was related to their job. On the other hand, a particular major might not provide certain characteristics at all. For example, English majors might not have been prepared for many activities they do not perform. Also, for some people in a particular major, there may be no relationship between attributes of the job or the education and the perception of relationship, even though there is variance in individual responses.

Tables 3.18 through 3.25 consider the variability of the relationship-defining variables by major. Table 3.18 provides responses to the question that is the most powerful defining variable. Although only 26 percent of social science majors, compared with over 60 percent of majors in certain other fields, use the content of majors almost always or frequently, quite a large number of respondents fall into almost all categories of frequency of use. This variability is one reason for the power of this factor.

For those majoring in English, other significant variables are: working with colleagues trained in the field; college training providing knowledge useful in the current job; and recommending one's major to others preparing for a similar job.

Table 3.19 indicates that few people in any major think their college education is not at all useful in providing the ability to think clearly. However, about half the respondents feel college is somewhat useful in this way, and half feel it is very useful. Regarding usefulness of college in providing knowledge and skills in current job, the most frequent response is "somewhat"; the least

TABLE 3.18

Use of Major Courses in Job, by Major (in percentages)

| Major | Use | | | | |
	Never	Rarely	Sometimes	Frequently	Almost Always
English	11	19	21	23	26
Arts and humanities	21	20	18	14	27
Economics	9	20	36	25	10
Social science	19	28	27	18	8
Natural science	10	16	19	26	29
Mathematics	7	22	32	20	19
Business	2	11	31	31	25
Education	4	8	20	35	33
Engineering	3	20	27	33	16
Other	6	9	17	22	46

frequent response is "not at all." For the variables analyzed in Tables 3.18, 3.19, and 3.20 variation in responses is substantial.

In almost all majors except business and engineering, a great majority (usually 75 percent) indicate that they are not supervising people trained in their fields (Table 3.21). About 60 percent (with education, engineering, and natural sciences lower) indicate they are not working with people trained in their field (Table 3.22). The restricted variation in these two factors probably accounts in part for their lower explanatory power.

TABLE 3.19

College Gave Ability to Think Clearly, by Major
(in percentages)

Major	Not at All	Somewhat	Very Much
English	3	51	46
Arts and humanities	4	54	42
Economics	4	47	49
Social science	4	52	44
Natural science	5	49	46
Mathematics	4	53	43
Business	4	58	38
Education	4	62	35
Engineering	2	40	58
Other	5	54	41

TABLE 3.20

College Gave Knowledge and Skills Used in Job, By Major
(in percentages)

Major	Not at All	Somewhat	Very Much
English	17	51	31
Arts and humanities	22	45	33
Economics	13	66	21
Social science	24	56	21
Natural science	13	41	45
Mathematics	13	58	30
Business	5	55	39
Education	9	40	51
Engineering	5	48	46
Other	9	34	56

Except for business and education, where more respondents recommend their major to others preparing for their job, approximately half of the respondents recommend their major (Table 3.23), and half do not. Similarly, about half use nonmajor courses on the job, and half do not (Table 3.24).

Table 3.25 presents the average number of activities for which college prepared respondents in various majors which they are not currently performing on their jobs. Although most respondents were prepared for only one or two activities not being used, 39 percent of business majors, 31 percent of engineering majors, and 28 percent of English majors were prepared for three or more

TABLE 3.21

Workers Who Supervise People in Field, by Major
(in percentages)

Major	Do Not Supervise People	Supervise People
English	84	16
Arts and humanities	91	9
Economics	75	25
Social science	85	15
Natural science	69	31
Mathematics	75	25
Business	58	42
Education	89	11
Engineering	57	43
Other	68	32

TABLE 3.22

Workers with Colleagues in and out of Own Field, by Major
(in percentages)

Major	Colleagues outside Field	Colleagues in Field
English	73	27
Arts and humanities	76	24
Economics	83	17
Social science	78	22
Natural science	64	36
Mathematics	71	29
Business	73	27
Education	32	68
Engineering	58	42
Other	63	37

TABLE 3.23

Workers Who Recommend Major for Job, By Major
(in percentages)

Major	Do Not Recommend Major	Recommend Major
English	46	54
Arts and humanities	47	53
Economics	55	45
Social science	47	53
Natural science	36	64
Mathematics	42	58
Business	16	84
Education	32	68
Engineering	20	80
Other	100	0

"useless" activities. Hence, even this variable might be highly significant for the pooled sample, although it might be less important in regressions focusing on specific majors. Actually, in all regressions except English and arts and humanities, this variable is significant, probably because small variations in the number of "useless" activities have a strong impact on individual perceptions of relationship.

In Table 3.17, for arts and humanities other than English, those indicating that their college education provided the ability to think clearly are less likely to perceive themselves as in closely related jobs. Those working with colleagues trained in their field, and those who feel that their college education provided useful knowledge are more likely to indicate that they are in closely related jobs. Those who recommend their major for their job are also more likely to be in closely related jobs. All four of these additional significant variables are consistent with the overall pattern. In economics, the only significant relationship variable is the use of the major. For social sciences other than economics, all except two of the defining variables are significant in the same way as the combined sample. The two insignificant variables are an indication that respondents supervise people trained in their fields and that they use courses other than those in their major. Here, it might be that social science majors are not in supervisory positions and use of other courses is infrequent.

For natural science majors, additional significant variables are an indication that college training provided knowledge useful in the current job, a recommendation of the major for those preparing for the job, working with colleagues in their field of training, and the number of activities they prepared for but do not perform. The signs of these variables are the same as those for

TABLE 3.24
Workers Who Use Content of Other Courses in Job, by Major (in percentages)

Major	Do Not Use Content	Use Content
English	61	39
Arts and humanities	58	42
Economics	57	43
Social science	62	38
Natural science	56	44
Mathematics	71	29
Business	65	35
Education	56	44
Engineering	69	31
Other	53	47

the pooled sample. For those trained in mathematics, all variables have signs similar to those for the pooled sample, except the indication that respondents supervise people trained in their field and that other courses are used on the job, which are not significant. This is similar to the social sciences.

Business majors are more likely to think their education is related to their job if they indicate that they work with or supervise people trained in their field and recommend their major to people who want similar jobs, and less likely if they use the content of other courses or are prepared for activities they do not perform. Once again, this is consistent with the overall pattern. Education majors also show patterns similar to those of the pooled sample, except that the ability to think clearly and the supervisory variables are not significant. Education majors in supervisory positions are probably no longer teaching and, hence, no longer using the content of their major. Engineering majors have a pattern similar to that of the pooled sample, in that all seven of the eight proposed variables appear significant. The ability to think clearly is not significant for this group.

Table 3.26 indicates the increment in the R^2s which results from adding the background and other variables in the regressions for particular majors. Although the general conclusion is that these variables, in addition to the relationship-defining variables, do not add much to the explanatory power of the model, in English, mathematics, and education these additional variables have the most incremental explanatory power. These three fields probably show the greatest dichotomy between those who specifically use their training and those in jobs very much unrelated to the college major. Whether or not English or mathematics majors, in particular, enter related jobs probably depends, more

TABLE 3.25

Number of Activities College Prepared Workers for Which Are
Unused on Job, by Major (in percentages)

	Activities			
Major	1–2	3–4	5–6	7–21
English	71	22	4	2
Arts and humanities	81	14	4	1
Economics	72	19	7	1
Social science	74	20	4	1
Natural science	73	21	5	1
Mathematics	76	19	5	0
Business	61	26	11	2
Education	78	18	3	1
Engineering	69	23	5	3
Other	76	18	4	1

than in other fields, on personal characteristics. In almost all cases, the final
set of variables adds virtually nothing, and the increment beyond the defining
variables comes from the addition of the personal and job characteristic variables.

DIFFERENCES BY OCCUPATION

Although congruence between certain occupations and certain majors is
substantial, Table 3.27 presents the simple relationship-defining regressions
separately for certain occupations. This table can be compared with Table 3.6,
which attempts to explain relationship by job level variables. Clearly, the
defining variables have much greater power in explaining relationship.

As in the regressions by major and sex, the use of major is always highly
significant. Although working with colleagues trained in one's field is significant in the regression by major, this variable is not significant for the occupations of allied health, computer programming and science, social work, and
secretary. In the first three cases, almost all colleagues are probably similarly
trained, whereas for secretaries, this variable is irrelevant. As in the regressions
by major, ability to think clearly is negatively related to the dependent variable,
but here it is significantly negative only for secretaries and teachers.

For those in administration, all other relationship-defining variables are
significant as in the pooled case except for "useless." For teachers, all variables
are significant except for the supervisory variable. In this case, the coefficient
is negative but not statistically significant, probably because few teachers are

TABLE 3.26

R²s at Each Step for Defining Relationship Subjectively, by Major

Step	English	Arts and Humanities	Eco- nomics	Social Science	Natural Science	Mathe- matics	Busi- ness	Educa- tion	Engineer- ing	Other
Relationship	.58	.70	.50	.56	.71	.49	.36	.56	.54	.62
Background	.68	.74	.53	.61	.74	.62	.40	.70	.60	.68
Other (final)	.69	.75	.54	.61	.74	.64	.41	.71	.60	.69

supervisors, and those who are feel they have moved out of the job that enabled them to use their training. Since such a large proportion of the sample is either in administration or teaching, this probably accounts for most of the patterns in the pooled regressions.

The lack of significance of the supervisory variable for those in allied health, computer, sales, secretarial, and social work might reflect the fact that people in these fields do not supervise. The lack of significance of the variable indicating college provided knowledge and skills for current job for many occupations probably reflects the fact that these jobs require learning by doing. In all cases except sales, where college does not provide useful knowledge, other undergraduate courses are not associated with relationship either. Finally, in all fields except communications and allied health, respondents who recommend their major are more likely to perceive its relationship to their job.

Table 3.27 and Table 3.6 support the conclusion that certain relationships between the defining variables and the dependent variable are specific to the nature of certain jobs, while others are more a function of major. However, the overall results appear quite strong.

CONCLUSION

One dimension that appears to determine the degree of relationship of education to job is the time of career selection. After eight years in the labor force, workers in occupations that require college-specific knowledge (for example, accountancy, allied health) are more likely to think their college education is very useful in their jobs than those in the more general college-prepared occupations. Two factors may be working here: occupations that require specific college training must be selected before or early in the college years; and certain jobs that do not require specific college training can be held either by those who are unable to find jobs that use their training or by individuals who were unable to select a curriculum to prepare themselves for a specific job. Certain jobs can be performed equally well with or without a college education, even if the general competencies required to complete college are also required for the job.

Few respondents indicated that no additional training is required beyond college. Most, however, indicated that most of their job skills are learned through on-the-job training. College is probably more beneficial in providing the foundation rather than the specific job competencies for building a career.

Another dimension of relationship is job level. It was conjectured that perhaps those in higher-level jobs, who think they have sufficient status and prestige, would consider their jobs more related to their college education. However, little individual difference in relationship was explained by the five

TABLE 3.27

Independent Variables Defining Relationship Subjectively, by Occupation
(betas in final step)

Variable	Administration (Middle, Business, Government)	Allied Health	Computer Programming and Science	Communications Specialist	Engineering	Sales	Secretary	Social Welfare	Teaching
Use content of major courses	.544*	.662	.522*	.569*	.352*	.654*	.648*	.548*	.523*
Colleagues work in my field	.104*	.062	.090	.180*	.203*	.088*	.082	.074	.169*
Recommend my major for my job	.132*	.098	.199*	.015	.160*	.142*	.174*	.204*	.083*
College taught knowledge and skills used in my job	.076*	.139*	.086	.087	.236*	.051	-.035	.078	.092*
Number of work activities college prepared but not doing	-.044	-.081	-.070	.021	-.052	-.037	.026	-.066	-.088*
Use content of courses other than major	-.125*	-.065	.041	-.099	-.120*	-.145*	.080	-.074	-.118*
College increased ability to think clearly	-.009	-.004	.002	-.065	.020	-.029	-.140*	-.103	-.066*
Supervise people trained in my field	.157*	.061	.024	.146*	.126*	-.020	.024	.057	-.028
N	794	172	217	115	288	315	109	123	1,265
R^2	.522	.602	.499	.543	.440	.500	.607	.472	.353

*Significant at .05 level.

variables indicating job level. It was also revealed that more women than men are in low-level jobs.

In defining an education-related job, the most powerful variable was the frequency of use of the content of major courses. The more frequently workers use their major courses in their jobs, the more likely they are to report that their job is closely related. Education majors use the content of their major most frequently, then business, natural sciences, and engineering majors. The content of their minor courses is also used most frequently by education majors. In the occupations, administrators, educators, and "other" professionals use the content of their major frequently or almost always regardless of their major.

Also contributing to perceptions of being in a closely related job are: recommending the major as preparation for the job; thinking college education provided knowledge useful in the current job; and working with or supervising people trained in the same field. Consequently, the relation of job to major depends not only on the use of major-course content, but also on the provision by college of a wider set of competencies.

The greater the number of activities for which college prepared an individual but which are not being performed on the current job, the less likely that that individual will indicate that his college major is closely related to his current job. If one goal of college training is to provide an education that will be perceived as related to later work, then it does not seem necessary to prepare an individual to perform a broad set of skills in addition to the skills and knowledge acquired from his concentration and from the more general college experience.

Significant differences were found between the male and female perceptions of relationship. Although the greatest factor for both groups is the frequency of use of content of major courses, the next most important factors for men are recommending their major and reporting that the knowledge obtained in college is useful on the current job. For women, however, the next most important factor is working with colleagues who were trained in their field.

Even after the addition of other background, education, and job variables, the relationship-defining variables remain highly significant and the significant differences between the men and the women persist.

There is a large range in the variance explained by the relationship-defining variables across majors and occupations. In each major and occupation regression, not all relationship variables appear significant. In fact, only one is significant across all regressions: frequency of use of content of major courses.

4

THE RELATIONSHIP OF
COLLEGE TO CAREER OUTCOMES

On one level, the concern that college education be applicable to the world of work is justifiable. If students are led into college and into particular programs expecting that what they learn will be useful on a job, the failure of this expectation to materialize implies imperfections in the economic or educational system. However, since demands for workers with particular skills fluctuate, it is wise to inform college students about the probabilistic nature of the job market and to suggest curricula that provide flexibility rather than specific skill training. And, if the effects of college extend beyond work, one must ask whether it is general college experience or specific curricula that best serve these purposes. Clearly, it costs more to produce a graduate trained in a laboratory science than one in humanities. Hence, if the overall payoffs (including payoffs unrelated to the job market) are invariate by major, then one might argue that individuals should major in the least expensive fields.

People interpret the meaning of usefulness of education or work differently. Whether individuals who, in whatever sense, believe they are using their college education in their jobs have more satisfactory career outcomes (for example higher job satisfaction and income) than those who felt otherwise is a question for investigation. That the answer is "yes" underlies much recent literature on the potential for revolution in this country led by underemployed college graduates who are discontent with their careers and lives. Even though the 1965 graduates we are studying cannot speak for the experiences of the class of 1975, it is crucial that we know how those already well established in the labor force use their training. By seeing whether or not utilization of training is related to job satisfaction and income of this group, we might infer effects of utilization on more recent graduates.

JOB SATISFACTION

The variance is great in the proportion of people in different majors very satisfied in different types of occupations. Table 4.1 presents the proportion of respondents with a particular major in a particular occupation who are very satisfied in their jobs. Data are given only where there are at least ten people with a particular major in an occupation. Although 87 percent of history majors in middle-level administration are very satisfied with their jobs, only 8 percent of majors in the arts are very satisfied. Whereas 80 percent of the social science majors working in business administration are very satisfied, only 7 percent working as secretaries are very satisfied. On one hand, it appears that individuals working in business administration, those who own their own businesses, and many in sales are very satisfied with their jobs, regardless of college major. On the other hand, one cannot say that certain major fields turn out individuals who are very satisfied regardless of their occupation. Although certain occupations are relatively distasteful regardless of major, even in these some job-holders are very satisfied. All jobs are liked by some people, even though no jobs are liked by all people.

As indicated before, a larger proportion of men than women think their jobs fit long-range goals: 56 percent of men and 37 percent of women (Table 2.1). Most people are satisfied with their jobs, regardless of relative pay. However, of those not satisfied, over 70 percent say they are not well paid. When respondents compared their salaries with those of others in the same occupation, with the same employer, and with the same education, the most important determinant of satisfaction was comparison with the same educational level. Table 4.2 presents the relationship between relative earnings and job satisfaction.

To what extent does relationship of job to major affect job satisfaction and income? Table 4.3 shows a relatively high degree of job satisfaction in the sample regardless of the relation of jobs to major. In one exception to this trend, those involuntarily in jobs not closely related to college major are significantly less satisfied. However, those voluntarily in closely related, somewhat related, or unrelated jobs are equally satisfied. Few individuals involuntarily hold jobs not closely related to their major. Roughly 60 percent of those voluntarily in closely related and unrelated jobs are very satisfied with their occupation. Those involuntarily holding somewhat related jobs are less satisfied (only 33 percent are very satisfied), while those holding jobs unrelated to their major are very satisfied and one-quarter are not at all satisfied.

Of course there are many other determinants of job satisfaction. However, the attempt here was not to develop the ultimate model of job satisfaction or income determination. The purpose of the following regressions was to see the extent to which relationship variables affect the two dependent variables. Some factors known or hypothesized to affect individual differences in income or job satisfaction were not included. However, the omission of important correlates with income and job satisfaction biases the results in a direction opposed to the hypotheses. The variables included, particularly some of the relationship variables, are probably correlated with some of the variables omitted. Some of the significance the model attributes to the included variables would be more appropriately attributable to some of the excluded variables. If the variables with which this study is concerned add little to the explanatory power of the model, then it can be anticipated that, had additional variables been included, the power of the variables upon which the study focuses would be even less. Only if some of the omitted variables were suppressor variables would it be possible to observe the relationship variables increasing in explanatory power after the addition of the omitted variables.

In regressions to explain satisfaction and income—specifically to discover the contribution of relationship-defining variables after controlling for other determinants—certain groups of variables were forced to enter the explanatory model in a specified order.* The first step was an attempt to explain income and job satisfaction by background variables related to personal and education characteristics and the sector in which the respondent was employed. These variables included sex, marital status, grade-point average, selectivity of institution, and the number of graduate courses taken in addition to courses required for the bachelor's degree. Data also included time when respondent chose his occupation, time spent with current employer, whether he is currently working or worked in the past, and years employed full time. In addition, dummy variables indicated whether the respondent was employed by a business firm, heavy industry, an educational institution, or the government. The coefficients on these employment-sector variables reflect differences in job satisfaction or income for individuals in particular sectors compared with those in the sector designated "other," which includes social service.

One alternative way to measure relationship would be to represent it by a trichotomous variable of responses to the question, "How closely related is your job to your college major?" As Table B.4 demonstrates, more individual differences in both income and job satisfaction can be explained by the defining variables than by responses to the direct question.

The approach selected has an additional advantage. By including defining variables, or the components of the perception of relationship, the aspects of a related job which contribute to workers' satisfaction can be understood. The perception of holding a job related to one's college training is affected by a variety of job and educational characteristics. It is valuable to understand

---

*We measure relationship by looking at the set of relationship-defining variables discussed in Chapter 3.

TABLE 4.1

Respondents Very Satisfied with Job, by Occupation and Major
(in percentages with N in parentheses)

Occupation	English	Foreign Languages	Arts	Eco-nomics	Soci-ology	Psychol-ogy	History	Social Science	Bio-logical Science
Accountant	—	—	—	48	—	—	—	—	—
	—	—	—	(23)	—	—	—	—	—
Middle administrator	73	50	8	28	64	33	87	41	—
	(22)	(10)	(13)	(18)	(14)	(15)	(28)	(17)	—
Business administrator	67	—	70	79	47	62	68	80	74
	(30)	—	(10)	(47)	(15)	(16)	(26)	(30)	(19)
Government administrator	50	—	—	—	—	27	60	53	54
	(12)	—	—	—	—	(11)	(10)	(17)	(11)
Allied health	—	—	—	—	—	—	—	—	48
	—	—	—	—	—	—	—	—	(63)
Architect	—	—	—	—	—	—	—	—	—
	—	—	—	—	—	—	—	—	—
Business owner	—	—	80	83	—	—	—	—	82
	—	—	(10)	(24)	—	—	—	—	(11)
Buyer	—	—	—	—	—	—	—	—	—
	—	—	—	—	—	—	—	—	—
Computer programmer	—	—	—	—	—	—	—	—	—
	—	—	—	—	—	—	—	—	—
Computer scientist	—	—	—	73	—	—	—	—	—
	—	—	—	(11)	—	—	—	—	—
Conservationist	—	—	—	—	—	—	—	—	62
	—	—	—	—	—	—	—	—	(13)
Communications specialist	11	—	44	—	—	—	—	70	—
	(27)	—	(9)	—	—	—	—	(10)	—
Counselor	60	—	—	—	—	—	—	—	—
	(5)	—	—	—	—	—	—	—	—
Artist	—	—	41	—	—	—	—	—	—
	—	—	(17)	—	—	—	—	—	—
Engineer	—	—	—	—	—	—	—	—	—
	—	—	—	—	—	—	—	—	—
Farmer	—	—	—	—	—	—	—	—	—
	—	—	—	—	—	—	—	—	—
Military	—	—	—	—	—	—	—	80	—
	—	—	—	—	—	—	—	(5)	—
Sales	14	—	62	74	68	58	52	62	62
	(15)	—	(21)	(35)	(19)	(24)	(23)	(21)	(16)
Natural scientist	—	—	—	—	—	—	—	—	28
	—	—	—	—	—	—	—	—	(28)
Secretary	19	23	28	—	27	0	12	7	—
	(21)	(13)	(14)	—	(11)	(11)	(17)	(14)	—
Social welfare	40	—	—	—	74	30	—	—	—
	(15)	—	—	—	(58)	(23)	—	—	—
Teacher	51	43	42	57	51	34	46	39	40
	(185)	(76)	(102)	(14)	(35)	(32)	(84)	(38)	(52)
Professor	—	—	—	—	—	—	—	—	—
	—	—	—	—	—	—	—	—	—
Technician	—	—	—	—	—	—	—	—	21
	—	—	—	—	—	—	—	—	(14)
Other	38	54	54	64	63	52	38	64	55
	(39)	(22)	(41)	(31)	(30)	(31)	(33)	(28)	(31)

Mathematics	Chemistry	Physics	Other Physical Sciences	Accounting	Business Administration	Business	Architecture	Education	Engineering	Other
—	—	—	—	56	43	—	—	—	—	—
—	—	—	—	(117)	(30)	—	—	—	—	—
—	—	—	—	—	23	—	—	—	—	—
—	—	—	—	—	(39)	—	—	—	—	—
79	60	—	—	66	71	—	—	—	82	60
(19)	(10)	—	—	(32)	(118)	—	—	—	(33)	(20)
—	—	—	—	—	58	—	—	—	—	—
—	—	—	—	—	(19)	—	—	—	—	—
—	56	—	—	—	—	—	—	—	—	52
—	(34)	—	—	—	—	—	—	—	—	(54)
—	—	—	—	—	—	—	92	—	—	—
—	—	—	—	—	—	—	(13)	—	—	—
—	—	—	—	78	78	—	—	—	—	—
—	—	—	—	(9)	(50)	—	—	—	—	—
—	—	—	—	—	57	—	—	—	—	—
—	—	—	—	—	(14)	—	—	—	—	—
48	—	—	—	—	—	—	—	—	—	—
(23)	—	—	—	—	—	—	—	—	—	—
46	—	—	—	—	38	—	—	—	46	—
(58)	—	—	—	—	(13)	—	—	—	(13)	—
—	—	—	—	—	—	—	—	—	—	—
—	—	—	—	—	—	—	—	—	—	—
—	—	—	—	—	—	—	—	—	—	54
—	—	—	—	—	—	—	—	—	—	(26)
—	—	—	—	—	—	—	—	—	—	—
—	—	—	—	—	—	—	—	—	—	—
—	—	—	—	—	—	—	—	—	—	—
—	—	—	—	—	—	—	—	—	—	—
69	—	30	100	—	—	—	—	—	45	—
(16)	—	(20)	(2)	—	—	—	—	—	(212)	—
—	—	—	—	—	—	—	—	—	—	75
—	—	—	—	—	—	—	—	—	—	(12)
—	—	—	—	—	69	—	—	—	87	—
—	—	—	—	—	(13)	—	—	—	(15)	—
73	—	—	—	—	69	—	—	69	60	70
(11)	—	—	—	—	(59)	—	—	(13)	(15)	(20)
50	—	—	—	—	—	—	—	—	—	—
(42)	—	—	—	—	—	—	—	—	—	—
—	—	—	—	—	20	—	—	—	—	0
—	—	—	—	—	(10)	—	—	—	—	(10)
—	—	—	—	—	—	—	—	—	—	—
—	—	—	—	—	—	—	—	—	—	—
52	—	—	—	—	65	73	—	60	—	60
(89)	—	—	—	—	(20)	(11)	—	(485)	—	(94)
—	—	—	—	—	—	—	—	—	—	83
—	—	—	—	—	—	—	—	—	—	(12)
—	—	—	—	—	—	—	—	—	—	—
—	—	—	—	—	—	—	—	—	—	—
53	64	—	90	—	54	—	—	61	67	49
(19)	(22)	—	(10)	—	(46)	—	—	(28)	(18)	(47)

TABLE 4.2

Relation of Earnings to Job Satisfaction
(in percentages)

| | Earnings | | |
Satisfaction	Well Paid, Compared with Others with Same Employer	Well Paid, Compared with Others with Other Employer	Well Paid, Compared with Others with Same Education
Not satisfied	3	36	60
Somewhat satisfied	4	32	64
Very satisfied	3	31	66

TABLE 4.3

Job Satisfaction, by Relationship Index
(in percentages)

Job Satisfaction	Closely Related	Somewhat Related		Not at All Related	
		Voluntary	Involuntary	Voluntary	Involuntary
Very satisfied	61	59	33	57	26
Somewhat satisfied	37	39	58	39	49
Not at all satisfied	3	2	9	4	26
Total	101	100	100	100	101

Source: A. S. Bisconti and L. C. Solomon, "The Utilization of Postsecondary Education in Careers," a study for the National Institute of Education and the College Placement Council, Inc., in progress.

which of these is linked to job satisfaction, since they all are significant in explaining the perception of relationship.

Creating a variable based on responses to the "how closely related" question and considering reasons why those in unrelated jobs are holding them (Chapter 3) enables five dummy variables to be developed, indicating the extent of relationship of job to major and whether those in relatively unrelated jobs are holding them voluntarily or involuntarily. The five-dummy possibility was eliminated because the direction of causation between these variables and job satisfaction was unclear. Those who hold satisfying jobs might indicate that they are holding them voluntarily and those in unsatisfying jobs that they are holding them involuntarily, with the direction of causation running from job satisfaction to perception of voluntary or involuntary reasons for holding a job. The choice was between the three-way response to the relationship question or the set of defining variables.

Table B.4 demonstrates that the greatest explanatory power would have come with the addition of the five dummy variables rather than the defining variables. However, this line of investigation was not pursued since it seemed clear that the effect of job satisfaction on perceptions was as great as the perception of voluntarily holding a job on job satisfaction.

After forcing in the relationship-defining variables, a set of dummies was inserted indicating the respondent's occupation and college major. Entry was limited to those with significant F values at the time (significant at the .05 level). It was hypothesized that job satisfaction and income could be a function of either occupation or major, in addition to other variables. After income was forced in to see if it affected job satisfaction, other variables dealing with values of college, excluded from the set of definitional variables, were used. These included indications that college education provided the respondent with leadership skills, the ability to choose life goals, and skills for his first job. Another set of variables, including responses to questions about whether college improved chances of finding a good job or provided skills for a first job, and whether the B.A. was a factor in being hired for the current job, served as a check to see whether the inclusion criteria were biasing the results. Finally, a set of additional variables, considered an indication of job characteristics (Does the respondent have policy responsibility? Is he/she self-employed? Does he/she design own program of work?), was included. These were hypothesized to affect job satisfaction independent of whether the respondent is holding a related job. As with the occupation and major dummies, the additional relationship factors and job traits only entered the regression if they were significant at the time of entry.

One variable not included in the relationship-defining set was an indication of whether the respondent thought his skills were being fully utilized on the job. This variable was allowed to enter the regression as the last step if it was significant. Its behavior demonstrated the point above. Skills fully utilized was excluded for two reasons.

First, this question was probably viewed as referring to a broader set of talents than those acquired in college. Hence, responses could not be interpreted as referring only to skills acquired in college—the focus of this study. Table 4.4 presents simple correlations between responses concerning full-skill utilization and other relationship variables, as well as job characteristics. For men, whether or not skills are fully utilized is not significantly correlated with any relationship-defining variables. For women, it is significantly correlated with only three relationship variables: that college provided knowledge useful in the current job, that the respondent uses the content of major courses in the job, and that college helped in choosing life goals. The latter can only be viewed as a relationship variable in a general sense. Skills fully utilized certainly does not refer only to college-acquired skills for men respondents, and probably refers to more than college-acquired skills for women. The interpretation clearly differs by sex of respondent. The correlation between utilization and

TABLE 4.4

Simple Correlations between Skills Fully Utilized, Relationship Variables, and Other College and Job Variables, by Sex

Variable	Correlation with Skills Fully Utilized		
	Total	Men	Women
Relationship			
College increased ability to think clearly	.047	.064	.020
College taught knowledge and skills used in current job	.199*	.172	.234*
Use content of major courses	.215*	.168	.273*
Supervise people in my field	.106	.142	.071
Colleagues in my field	.156	.121	.191
Recommend major as preparation for my job	.080	.066	.108
Use content of other undergraduate courses	.121	.105	.136
Number of work activities college prepared, but not doing	−.079	−.056	−.112
Other			
College increased general knowledge	.033	−.014	.022
College increased leadership ability	.063	.044	.086
College taught skill that helped get my first job	.142	.104	.186
College increased my chances of finding a good job	.109	.089	.136*
College helped me choose my life goals	.155	.120	.199*
B.A. was a factor in hiring	.070	.033	.129
B.A. was necessary for promotion	.034	.024	.053
College provided contacts which enabled me to get current job	.078	.046	.117
I set my own hours	.062	.107	.013
I design my own work program	.092	.105	.090
Have policy and decision-making responsibility	.140	.181	.128
Am self-employed	.057	.088	.099
Job satisfaction	.302*	.300*	.323*
Relation of job to major	.204*	.167	.251*
Salary	.018	.067	.078

*Significant at .05 level.

the variable indicating how closely related one's job is to major is .204, statistically significant for women but not for men. Nevertheless, the correlation between fully utilized skills and job satisfaction is .302, statistically significant for both men and women. Job satisfaction derives from the perception that many talents beyond those acquired in college are used in work.

The second reason for excluding responses to the question, Are your skills fully utilized? from the set of relationship-defining variables was the circular nature of its effect: It may be that people who are satisfied indicate that their skills are fully utilized rather than that people whose skills are fully utilized indicated job satisfaction. If the direction of causation runs both ways, the variable should have much explanatory power. After controlling for all other factors, skills fully utilized had a large impact on job satisfaction. However, this variable had an insignificant correlation with income. Apparently, those who earn a great deal think they have many skills in addition to those utilized.

The research focuses first on job satisfaction as the dependent variable, then on income regressions separately by sex, since there were significant sex differences.* The regressions are presented after all the background and relationship-defining variables were forced to enter the regression (before the other variables entered). This enabled a focus on the background and relationship factors, although the omitted variables bias the results toward artificially increasing the significance of the background and defining variables. However, beta weights from the last step—after all variables are entered—are also presented, as is a list of "significant other" variables with their signs which entered later.

Table 4.5 shows the proportion of variance explained after successive groups of variables entered into the job-satisfaction regression. The combination of variables included in the model explain approximately 20 percent of the individual differences in job satisfaction of men and women. Moreover, after controlling for background factors, the variables suggested as components or relationship contribute .017 to the R^2 for men and .034 to the R^2 for women. Of course, since some multicolinearity between groups of variables exists, the later in the sequencing that relationship-defining variables enter, the smaller their contribution to R^2. The addition to R^2 contributed by the relationship-defining variables is statistically significant ($F= 11.96$, significant at the .01 level). However, contributions of this magnitude do not have important policy implications in terms of the importance of relationship for increasing job satisfaction. In models with thousands of observations, even the most inconsequential changes can be statistically significant. Nevertheless, the perception

---

*According to the Chow test, calculated after the relationship step, $F = 3.15$ for the job satisfaction regressions, and $F= 8.61$ for the income regressions—both significant at the .01 level.

TABLE 4.5

R²s in Job Satisfaction Regressions, by Step

Step	Total	Men	Women
Background	0.046	0.060	0.047
Relationship	0.067	0.077	0.081
Occupation	0.099	0.107	0.109
Major	0.103	0.111	0.116
Income	0.116	0.130	0.123
Other college-education variables	0.128	0.142	0.135
Other job variables	0.149	0.170	0.143
Skills fully utilized	0.200	0.217	0.206
N	4,291	2,688	1,603

of relationship of job to major is a more important factor in determining job satisfaction of women than of men. The addition of dummy variables indicating occupations and majors added about the same amount to the power of the model as the addition of the relationship variables. Income contributed a relatively small amount (about .015 percentage points).

The inclusion of other perceptions of the contribution of college, which did not warrant inclusion in the definition of relationship, added little to the explanatory power of the model. The individual differences in three postulated job characteristics increased the R^2 for men by .028 and for women by .008, an indication that autonomy is both more important to and more frequently achieved by men than women. An indication that the respondent thought his skills were fully utilized on the job was allowed to enter last. After considering all previously entering variables, this factor still added substantially to the explanatory power of the model. The increase in R^2 for men was .047, for women .063. There may be a two-way influence on this variable, that is, rather than fully utilized skills leading to job satisfaction, those satisfied in their jobs are probably more likely to think their skills are fully utilized. The power of this variable in the job-satisfaction regressions contrasts with its insignificance in explaining individual differences in income.

Table 4.6 presents the results of the regression estimates to explain individual differences in job satisfaction for men and women. The first column for each sex provides the beta weights after the background and relationship-defining variables have entered. The second column for each sex indicates the coefficient in the final step after all other variables have been allowed to enter if significant. The table also lists those variables in addition to the background and relationship sets which are significant in the final step of the regression.

For men, three background variables affect satisfaction at both stages of the analyses: The longer a man has been employed full time, the more satisfied he

TABLE 4.6

Job Satisfaction Regression with Relationship Variables, by Sex

Variable	Men (N = 2,688)		Women (N = 1,603)	
	Beta after Relationship Step	Final Beta	Beta after Relationship Step	Final Beta
Background				
College grade-point average	−.008	−.009	.013	.000
Selectivity of institution	−.001	−.026	−.003	.006
When occupation was chosen	.009	.003	.010	.056
Number of years experience with current employer	−.016	−.022	.115*	.106*
Have worked in past, not now	−.115*	−.097*	−.121*	−.085*
Years employed full time	.098*	.055*	.013	−.031
Number of graduate courses taken	−.038	−.025	−.033	−.032
Business firm employer	−.027	−.043	.067*	.041
Heavy industry employer	−.074*	−.025	.042	.055*
Education employer	−.102*	−.048	.002	−.006*
Government employer	−.079*	−.032	.013	.004
Single	.004	.034	−.004*	−.047
Married	.105*	.089*	.056	.036
Relationship				
College increased ability to think clearly	.071*	.040*	.023	.000
College taught knowledge and skills used in current job	.062*	.031	.085*	.043
Use content of major courses	.030	.002	.085*	.038
Supervise people in my field	.016	−.039*	.001	−.016
Colleagues in my field	−.003	.014	.067*	.019
Recommended major as preparation for my job	.008	.007	−.028	−.048*
Use content of other undergraduate courses	.036	.009	.089*	.070*
Number of work activities college prepared, but not doing	−.024	−.008	.015	.047*

*Significant at .05 level.

For men: Other variables significant in the final step and their signs were office work occupation (−), engineering occupation (−), accountant (−), English major (−), economics major (+), salary (+), college helped choose life goals (+), B.A. was factor in hiring (−), college increased chances of finding a good job (+), have policy and decision-making responsibility (+), am self-employed (+), design own work program (+), skills are fully utilized in my job (+), and B.A. was necessary for promotion (+). Other variables not significant in the final step were mathematics and science occupation, social work, and other professional occupations.

For women: Other variables significant in the final step and their signs were administrators (+), other professional occupations (+), education occupations (+), education major (+), salary (+), college increased chances of finding a good job (+), college increased leadership ability (+), design own program (+), and skills are fully utilized in job (+). Other variables not significant in final step were office work occupation, sales, have policy decision-making responsibility.

is. This confirms that older or more experienced workers are more satisfied than younger workers. Married men tend to be more satisfied than single, divorced, or widowed men. Men who worked in the past but who are no longer working are less satisfied than those currently employed.

For men, a number of dummy variables tied to the employment sector initially appeared significant, indicating that men in heavy industry, education, and government are significantly less satisfied than those in business firms or other sectors, primarily social services. However, after the other variables entered, these factors no longer seemed significant in the final step. Variables that entered later considered specific majors and individual occupations, so these sector variables no longer reflected occupation and major.

For women, the more years of experience, the more satisfied the respondent with her job. The effect here is the same as the variable for men of years employed full time. Those not currently employed are less satisfied than those still employed—also similar to men. For women employed by business firms, job satisfaction is greater than for those in other sectors. However, this effect becomes statistically insignificant once the major and occupation are inserted, although in the final step, women employed in heavy industry appear more satisfied than those in other sectors.

Grade-point average, selectivity of college, and time when occupation was chosen never affect job satisfaction for either men or women. Marital status never affects job satisfaction for women. At all stages for both sexes, there is an insignificant negative coefficient on the number of graduate courses taken, possibly indicating an attempt by those less satisfied to obtain additional credentials to change jobs. It is also possible that these respondents had to lower their expectations because they did not finish their graduate work.

Background variables explain no more than 6 percent of the individual differences in job satisfaction for either men or women. Apparently other factors are more important, since the complete set of variables explains over 20 percent of individual differences.

There were significant sex differences in the effects of the relationship-defining variables on individual job satisfaction. Table 4.5 shows only .017 percentage points added to the R^2 for men, but .034 added for women. In part, the explanation is that only two of the relationship-defining variables were initially significant in the male regression, whereas four had significant effects on female differences in job satisfaction.

Men and women, who indicated that their college education provided skills and knowledge useful in their current jobs are more satisfied. Do "skills and knowledge" include only the substance of courses, or does use of general college experiences add to job satisfaction? Several clues help answer this question.

For men, the use of content of major or other courses on the job does not affect job satisfaction. However, women who use their major and other courses are more satisfied, that is, these variables are statistically significant, as is the indication that college provided useful skills and knowledge. The satisfaction resulting from the provision of skills and knowledge for men probably refers to knowledge of the substance of major and other courses, whereas for women this variable refers to competencies in addition to substance of courses.

Table 4.7 shows that the correlation between "use of content of major" and the indication that college provided skills and knowledge useful in the job is higher for men than for women (.606 versus .502). For men, the latter has a higher partial correlation, after controlling for the background variables, with job satisfaction, than the former (.094 versus .065). For women, the partial between job satisfaction and indication that college provided skills and knowledge is the same as the partials between job satisfaction and use of major course and job satisfaction and use of other courses (.126). For men, the significance of the "skills and knowledge" variable is picking up (or representing) the significance of the "use of major" variable, whereas, for women, the "skills and knowledge" variable stands for something different than the use of specific course content.

The relationship component variables add little to the ability of the model to explain individual differences in job satisfaction. However, men do appear more satisfied only if they think they are using course content on their job, whereas women get more job satisfaction not only by using course content, but also if they think college provided additional skills and knowledge used at work. To speculate, these other competencies might include competitiveness and leadership skills, probably acquired earlier in life by more men than women; work habits; learning how to learn; and others.

Several other relationship-defining variables were significant at the time the set entered. Changes also appeared by the final step of the regression. In addition to skills and knowledge, men who feel that college provides the ability to think clearly are more satisfied with their jobs. Whether individuals supervise people or work with colleagues trained in their field, are trained for activities they do not do or recommend their major as preparation for their job has no effect on job satisfaction.

After adding the remaining variables, an indication that college experience provided knowledge useful in the current job was no longer significant. However, the indication that college provided the ability to think clearly remained a statistically significant factor in explaining job satisfaction of men. In the final step, there was a significantly negative relationship between supervising people trained in one's field and job satisfaction, implying that, after controlling for all other factors, those in relatively unrelated jobs were more satisfied.

Women who indicated that their colleagues were trained in their field tend to be more satisfied, suggesting that interpersonal relationships are more important for women.

TABLE 4.7

Intercorrelations of Job Satisfaction and Relationship Variables, by Sex

Variable	Partial r with Job Satisfaction Controlling for Background Variables	Job Satisfaction	Use Content of Major Courses	Use Content of Other Undergraduate Courses	Recommend Major as Preparation for My Job	College Taught Knowledge and Skills Used in Current Job
Men						
Job satisfaction	–	1.000	–	–	–	–
Use content of major courses	.079	.083	1.000	–	–	–
Use content of other undergraduate courses	.065	.059	.288	1.000	–	–
Recommended major as preparation for my job	.034	.041	.304	.040	1.000	–
College taught knowledge and skills used in current job	.094	.097	.606	.262	.256	1.000
Women						
Job satisfaction	–	1.000	–	–	–	–
Use content of major courses	.124	.140	1.000	–	–	–
Use content of other undergraduate courses	.126	.138	.317	1.000	–	–
Recommend major as preparation for my job	.004	.026	.269	.048	1.000	–
College taught knowledge and skills used in current job	.126	.172	.502	.265	.236	1.000

After adding the remaining variables to explain individual differences in job satisfaction of women, the significant relationship-defining variables changed. As with men, an indication that college provided knowledge useful in the current job no longer appears significant. Also losing significance is an indication that women use the content of the courses in their major and that colleagues were trained in their field.

In the job satisfaction regression for women, two variables gained significance by the time all had entered. In the final step, those women who recommended their major are less satisfied; the more activities for which college prepared women but which they are not using, the more satisfied they were. These two variables worked in an opposite direction for the regression. That is, those who recommended their major for job preparation are more likely to say they are in a related job; the fewer activities for which an individual was trained but is not performing, the more likely that individual is to indicate that she is in a related job. In addition, those who are using their nonmajor subjects are more likely than those who are not to indicate they are in an unrelated job.

These three factors, the only significant ones in the final step, indicate that there is a significant negative relationship between relationship and job satisfaction after other factors affecting satisfaction are introduced. Those women who end up in jobs least prepared for by college are most satisfied. This is not as surprising as it might appear, given the types of jobs women have traditionally prepared for during college. Whereas a man might have majored in business and taken an unrelated minor, a woman more typically would have majored in English and taken several business courses on the side. If business is a satisfying career, then one would expect a positive relationship between use of major (business) and satisfaction of a man working in business, but a negative relationship between use of major (English) and satisfaction of a woman in business. For women, one might also expect a positive relationship between use of nonmajor courses (if they are in business) and job satisfaction. The data show that those women not using their college major or nonmajor courses are more satisfied. However, this is not the case for men.

Table 4.6 describes other variables that entered the final step of the job satisfaction regressions. Office work, engineering, and accountancy are relatively unsatisfying occupations for men, whereas administration, other professional occupations (primarily social services), and education are satisfying occupations for women. Men who major in economics are significantly more satisfied with their jobs, while men who major in English are significantly less satisfied. For women, a major in education results in a more satisfying job than do other majors.

Despite its small contribution to the overall explanatory power of the model, salary has a significantly positive effect on job satisfaction for both men and women. Men who are self-employed, have policy responsibility, or design their own work programs are significantly more satisfied as well. However, women with policy responsibility are not significantly more satisfied, and the self-employment variable does not even enter the female regression. The insignificance of these last two factors for women indicates not that women do not find these characteristics important, but that there are almost no women whose jobs entail policy responsibility; there are almost no self-employed women.

Five college characteristics not included in the relationship-defining set of variables entered the regression later for men, but only three entered for women. For both men and women, a feeling that skills were fully utilized is associated with greater job satisfaction. As noted, a dual direction of causation was probably the reason for the power of this variable. For men, an indication that a bachelor's degree is a factor in being hired leads to lower job satisfaction. If the B.A. is still a credential ten years after they have entered the labor force, men are probably not attaining satisfactory jobs. Men who think that the B.A. improved their chances for finding a good job and was necessary for promotion are more satisfied. Apparently, college education is still serving certain indirect credentialing functions, leading to better jobs; for example, once hired, those without a degree do not get promoted. Finally, for men, those who think that college education helped them choose their life goals are more satisfied. This characteristic might have nothing to do with jobs directly, but it might indicate that when college enables individuals to make good decisions in their overall lives this ability leads to more satisfactory work relationships as well.

Women who think that college provided them with leadership skills they can exercise on their jobs are more satisfied. In the regression equation for women, those who indicated that college improved their chances of finding a good job are more satisfied. Apparently, those who have good jobs attribute part of the reason to their college education.

Table 4.6 indicates which aspects of relationship affect job satisfaction. Apparently, men are more satisfied when college courses provide useful facts that can be applied to work. However, characteristics of colleagues and the contribution of college in providing general knowledge do not seem to have a significant effect on job satisfaction of men. With all factors included, only an indication that college provided the ability to think clearly contributes to satisfaction. For women, it appeared at one stage of the analysis that the contribution of both specific course content and more general competencies contribute to job satisfaction. However, after controlling for other factors, including a particular major and occupation, women who hold jobs specifically unrelated to college are most satisfied. Other than providing general useful experiences, college does not affect job satisfaction of men and women. College training is something to avoid using to obtain a satisfactory job, particularly for women, who have traditionally been limited in the types of jobs for which they can seek preparation in college.

INCOME

Do those who use their college education earn more than those who do not, after controlling for a variety of other factors? There are a number of reasons why one would expect individuals using their college education to earn more. In particular, if college education enables one to be more productive in specific jobs, than those who are able to hold jobs requiring college-level skills should be more productive than individuals unable to use their acquired skills. Economists have argued that in general those who earn more are more productive. The education-income relationship, then, demonstrates that those of a given education level who are able to apply their learning are more productive and earn more income.

Much credentialing discussion has centered around the efficacy of the practice of paying more for individuals with higher levels of education; the assumption being that the more highly educated who are using their skills are more productive. Since all individuals in this study have the same amount of education—mainly a bachelor's degree—credentialing could be based on grade-point average, specific major, selectivity of institution, or other such criteria. It is possible to net out effects of all these factors to see whether those using their education are, indeed, earning more.

Table 4.8 calculates the contribution of the groups of variables to the model to explain individual differences in income. The complete set of independent variables served to explain 32 percent of individual income differences among men and 46 percent among women. The set of background variables is important in explaining individual differences in income. Specifically, the background characteristics explain as much of the individual differences in income as the full set of variables explain individual differences in job satisfaction. The background variables explain almost twice as many of the individual differences in income for women as for men.

TABLE 4.8

R^2s in Income Regressions at Each Step

Step	Total	Men	Women
Background	0.383	0.202	0.347
Relationship	0.400	0.229	0.359
Occupation	0.447	0.281	0.438
Major	0.454	0.290	0.446
Other college-education variables	0.458	0.296	0.448
Other job variables	0.474	0.322	0.452
Skills fully utilized in my job	(never came in)	(never came in)	0.455

Considering the background factors, relationship-defining variables add a small (even if statistically significant) amount to the power of the model to explain individual income differences. The eight defining variables contribute .027 points to the R^2 for men and .012 to the R^2 for women. With the many observations in the regressions, even the smallest increment to R^2 can be statistically significant. However, that the change in R^2 is significant still must be noted despite its small size. Individual differences in occupation and major add .061 to the R^2 for men and .087 for women. After allowing the occupation and major dummies to enter, the other perceived contributions of college add virtually nothing to R^2. For men, job characteristics, such as self-employment, policy responsibility, and opportunity to design one's own work program, add about .026 to the R^2, whereas for women these variables contribute only .004.

Finally, for men, the variable representing the perception that one's skills are utilized is not sufficiently significant to enter the equation at the end. Although this variable did enter for women, it added virtually nothing to the explanatory power of the model. Although fully utilizing skills is positively associated with job satisfaction, the perception that one's skills are fully utilized has no independent explanatory power in a model to explain individual income differences. The first observation—the association between full utilization of skills and job satisfaction—has already been explained by noting the circular nature of the possible causation. The insignificant relationship between the perception that one's skills are fully utilized and income can be explained by the observation that highly productive people are likely to feel that they have unused talents beyond those enabling them to earn high incomes.

Table 4.9 provides details of the income regressions. Although background variables explain less than 6 percent of individual differences in job satisfaction of men and women, they explain 20 percent of the differences in income of men and over 34 percent in income of women. This set of variables includes a number that were important determinants of income in earlier studies (Solmon 1975). In particular, college selectivity, years of experience, years employed full time, and marital status are positively associated with income for both men and women. Grade-point average is also associated with higher earnings for men. Single men make less, whereas single women make more, also a customary finding. For men, the earlier an occupation is chosen, the higher the income, implying that those who have had more time to prepare for their chosen careers generally choose careers with higher earnings. Several dummy variables indicating employment sector were significant in the final step of the regressions for both men and women, indicating that different sectors have differential pay scales. Almost all the variables retained their effects in the final step after all variables were allowed to enter. However, for men, the number of years of full-time employment was not initially significant but became significant by the final step; the same thing occurred with marital status. For

TABLE 4.9

Income Regression with Relationship Variables, by Sex

Variable	Men		Women	
	Beta after Relationship Step	Final Beta	Beta after Relationship Step	Final Beta
Background				
College grade-point average	.113*	.111*	.006	-.013
Selectivity of institution	.117*	.111*	.136*	.101*
When occupation was chosen	-.048*	-.080*	.017	.018
Number of years experience with current employer	.071*	.081*	.143*	.123*
Have worked in past, not now	-.034	-.022	-.177*	-.145*
Years employed full time	.140	.103*	.239*	.208*
Number of graduate courses taken	-.045	-.009	.025	.021
Business firm employer	.168	.064*	.097*	.043
Heavy industry employer	.082	.051*	.126*	.089*
Education employer	-.181	-.082*	-.107*	-.118*
Government employer	.007	.008	.108*	.083*
Single	-.094	-.069*	.085*	.052
Married	.025	.013	.069	.025
Relationship				
College increased ability to think clearly	.056*	.036*	-.004	.007
College taught knowledge and skills used in current job	-.006	.002	.002	-.029
Use content of major courses	-.035	-.057*	-.004	-.025
Supervise people in my field	.136*	.102*	.076*	.025
Colleagues in my field	-.041*	-.004	.038	.010
Recommend major as preparation for my job	.067*	.038*	.004	.005
Use content of other undergraduate courses	.017	.010	-.016	-.009
Number of work activities college prepared, but not doing	-.047*	-.042*	-.070*	-.056*

*Significant at .05 level.

For men: Other variables significant in the final step and their signs were administrator sales (+), accountant (+), allied health worker (+), other professional occupations (+), mathematics and science occupations (+), economics major (+), business major (+), engineer major (+), college increased chances of finding a good job (+), college taught skill that enabled me to get my first job (-), am self-employed (+), set own hours (+), and have policy decision-making responsibilities (+). Other variables not significant in the final step were B.A. was a factor in hiring, and college increased leadership ability.

For women: Other variables significant in the final step and their signs were administrator (+), mathematics and science occupations (+), sales (+), other professional occupations (+), education occupations (+), allied health worker (+), accountant (+), social worker (+), mathematics major (+), natural science major (-), B.A. was a factor in hiring (+), have policy and decision-making responsibilities (+), skills fully used in job (+), and B.A. was necessary for promotion (+). Other variables not significant in the final step were office work occupation and engineering occupation.

women, marital status had an effect initially but, after controlling for other factors, it was no longer important.

Despite the large contribution of the background factors, the additional variables to the income regressions contributed 10 more percentage points to the explanatory power of the model. However, the relationship variables contributed virtually none of this. Nevertheless, in the male regression, five of the relationship variables were significant concomitants with income at the time they entered and four retained their statistical significance in the final step.

Those who indicated that they supervise people trained in their field earn more than others. This finding might indicate that supervision alone is important rather than supervision of people in the same field. Those who think college education provided them with the ability to think more clearly earn more. Possibly, it is the general competencies provided by college which lead to higher income rather than the specific contribution of course content. Those who use the content of their major courses earn significantly less than others. However, the more things that college prepared one to do which he is not doing, the lower the income. Also, those who recommend their major for a job like theirs tend to earn more than others. These findings together might imply that those who recommend their major are not doing so with the intention that those studying their major will use the specific course content but, rather, that they will gain more general abilities that will lead to higher income. It is not the tasks that college prepares one to do which lead to higher income but, rather, the more general competencies that help with work even if not specifically applied on the job. Another possibility is that they may not feel the course content is related, but they may feel it is useful on the job. Overall, it appears that those men who think that college contributed in general ways to their competency are also those who earn higher incomes.

Far fewer of the relationship-defining variables are significant in explaining income differences for women. In the step after the relationship variables entered, an indication that a woman supervises people trained in her field is associated with higher income, but this association might simply indicate that supervisory jobs yield higher income. This variable is not significant in the final step. The only other variable significant in the earnings function for women, both at the end of the relationship step and in the final step, is the number of activities for which college trained a woman but which she is not using. As with men, the relationship here is negative, indicating that women trained to do many things they are not doing tend to earn less than others. This finding implies that to acquire a lot of skills in college which will not be used is counterproductive in an income-generating sense. However, this may be an artifact of particular occupations and will be explored in later chapters.

Of the other variables that enter into the earnings functions after the relationship-defining variables, many simply indicate which occupations are relatively high paying for men and women. For men, these occupations are administration, sales, accountancy, allied health, other professionals, and mathematical and scientific occupations. Women in administration, mathematics and science, sales and other professionals, allied health, accountancy, social work, and education tend to earn more. Men who majored in economics, business, and engineering earn more. Women who majored in mathematics make more, but those who majored in natural sciences make less.

Men who indicated that they are self-employed, set their own work hours, and have policy responsibility earn more, while women who indicated that they have policy responsibility earn more. That these other job characteristics do not enter the equation for women once again is probably because few women possess jobs with these characteristics, rather than because these characteristics are not associated with higher income for women.

Only two of the other potential values of college are significantly associated with income of men, whereas three are related to earnings of women. Men who say that their college education increased their chances of finding a good job tend to earn more, but the circular nature of this variable is evident. Men who say that college provided them with a skill useful in their first job tend to earn less. Men who think college served as a credential for their first job are probably unable to benefit from other noncollege skills that contribute to earnings as well. Women who think that the B.A. was important to their being hired and promoted tend to earn more. Apparently, women think the bachelor's degree is more important as a credential in terms of their earning ability than do men. Since some evidence indicates that they are discriminated against in hiring, women probably need the educational credential more than men who might be hired for other reasons. Women who think their skills are fully utilized tend to earn more. Apparently, women attribute higher earnings to full utilization of skills more often than men.

This study explains a good many of the individual differences in income of both men and women. However, the contribution of the relationship variables to this model is slight. For women, relationship-defining variables rarely enter the equation; for men the general contributions of college rather than the specific course content are more often associated with higher earnings. The particular occupation and major selected by workers seem more important than the interface between education and the particular job responsibilities.

JOB LEVEL

Earlier, this study hypothesized that job level might be a significant factor in perceptions of relationship. It was shown that job level did not have an important independent effect on this perception. Here the focus is on the extent to which job level affects job satisfaction. Although only 20 percent of individual differences in job satisfaction can be explained by the full set of variables

(Table 4.5), Table 4.10 explains 27 percent of individual differences in job satisfaction by the set of five variables alone. The five variables are highly correlated with and, indeed, part of the definition of job satisfaction.

An indication that one is making satisfactory career progress, that one has sufficient job status, and that one's skills are fully utilized are all positively associated with job satisfaction, as is high income. The perception that one is working at a professional level does not affect job satisfaction significantly. Table 4.10 also indicates a simple correlation between level variables and income and job satisfaction.

Table 4.11 provides data on the income level of individuals indicating that they have high-level jobs. Among the men, 69 percent think they have sufficient job status and, of these, 52 percent fall into the top third of the income distribution, while only 6 percent fall into the low third. Similarly, of the 68 percent of men who think they are working at a professional level, about 50 percent are in the high third of the income distribution. Only 31 percent think their skills are fully utilized, 49 percent in the high third and 8 percent in the low third of the income distribution.

Although approximately the same proportion of women think they have high-level jobs, where these individuals fall in the income distribution is quite different. A total of 61 percent think they have a job of sufficiently high status, but 56 percent of those have incomes in the low third of the income distribution, and only 6 percent have incomes in the high third. Similarly, 67 percent of the women think they are working at a professional level, but 53 percent are in the low income third. Skills are thought to be fully utilized by 35 percent, but 53 percent in the low income third and only 6 percent are in the high

TABLE 4.10

Predicting Job Satisfaction with Level Variables, and Their Correlations with Income and Job Satisfaction

Variable	Raw Beta in Final Step	Simple Correlation	
		Income	Job Satisfaction
R^2	.27	—	—
Income	.02*	—	.19*
Satisfied with career progress	.37*	.24*	.45*
Skills fully used in my job	.22*	.02	.30*
Have sufficient job status	.20*	.20*	.36*
Am working at professional level	.02	.13	.20*
Constant	1.14	—	—
N	5,119	—	—

*Significant at .01 level.

TABLE 4.11

Income and Job Level, by Sex
(in percentages)

Level Variable	Low Income	Middle Income	High Income	Percent Saying Yes
Men				
Have sufficient job status	6	41	52	69
Skills fully used in my job	8	44	49	31
Am working at professional level	6	44	50	68
Women				
Have sufficient job status	56	38	6	61
Skills fully used in my job	53	42	6	35
Am working at professional level	53	41	6	67

income third. Job level is much more a function of income for men than for women. Women can think they are in high-level jobs despite low income, where this is a rare occurrence indeed for men. Whether this is a rationalization because women are unable to obtain jobs among the highest paying is unclear.

The data partly explain the sizable individual differences in both job satisfaction and income. But the interface between education and work, particularly the specific application on the job of facts learned in college, does not have much impact on either job satisfaction or income. In short, a related job does not assure happiness and riches.

5

THE RELATIONSHIP OF
COLLEGE TO CAREER
OUTCOMES BY MAJOR

In considering income and job satisfaction outcomes of the interface between education and work, male and female differences are important. Since men and women have traditionally selected different majors, it is not unreasonable to suggest that substantial differences in these two outcomes may be found among individuals who have majored in different undergraduate fields or who have chosen various occupations. Perhaps job satisfaction for those who majored in English, economics, other social sciences, and education depends on how related the jobs are to the major fields of study. Those in business, engineering, and the natural sciences are more likely than those in the humanities, social sciences, and education to find related jobs in the current market and, therefore, relationship may be of less concern to them. Whether a job is related to the major may vary in importance as a determinant of job satisfaction according to major field. The following results are of the income and job satisfaction analyses by major field, with special emphasis on the effects of relationship variables.

For these analyses, responses to the question "In which area did you take the most courses for your undergraduate degree?" were grouped into five generic categories. The largest category, natural sciences and engineering, has 1,049 cases and includes biological sciences, mathematical sciences, chemistry, biochemistry, physics, earth science, engineering, and other physical sciences. The second largest category, economics and social sciences, has 1,032 cases. It includes economics, sociology, psychology, history, and other social sciences (for example, anthropology, geography, and political science).

Education is the smallest category with 456 cases. The other groups are business, with 688 cases, including accounting, business administration, and other business areas; and English and humanities, with 730 cases encompassing English, foreign languages, fine arts, music, philosophy, and other arts and humanities.

JOB SATISFACTION

In the stepwise multiple regressions explaining job satisfaction by major, six groups of independent variables were forced in. Table 5.1 summarizes these six steps. Since the concern is more one of explaining the relationship of college education to work and the level of job satisfaction than of developing a full model to explain job satisfaction, steps one and two in Tables 5.1 and 5.2 are of greater interest. As in the total regression, first all background variables were forced in, regardless of level of significance; then the eight relationship-defining variables were forced in—in the same manner—for each generic major regression. At the third step, income was forced in. The remaining variables were allowed in only if their entering F values were significant at the .05 level.

Economics and Other Social Science Majors

The background variables contribute a greater proportion of the variance in explaining individual differences in job satisfaction (8.6 percent) for this category of majors than for the other four categories (Table 5.1). Five background variables are important in relation to job satisfaction after the relationship step (Table 5.2). In Tables 5.2, 5.3, 5.6, and 5.7, a + means the variable is significantly related to greater job satisfaction, a − indicates a significant relationship to lower job satisfaction, and a zero signifies no relationship.

Important for greater job satisfaction for economics and other social science majors are being female, married, and being employed full time many years since graduation. Women report greater job satisfaction than men, regardless

TABLE 5.1

R²s in Job Satisfaction Regressions at Each Step, by Major

Step	Economics and Social Science (N = 1,032)	English and Humanities (N = 730)	Natural Sciences, Mathematics, and Engineering (N = 1,049)	Business (N = 688)	Education (N = 456)
Background	.086	.063	.075	.062	.064
Relationship	.111	.102	.095	.098	.121
Income	.132	.108	.128	.133	.128
Other education variables	—	.119	.166	.144	—
Other job variables	.167	.130	.189	.168	.173
Skills fully used	.213	.202	.237	.220	.216

TABLE 5.2

Important Variables Associated with Job Satisfaction after Relationship Step, by Major

Variable	Sign of Variable if Significant*				
	Economics and Social Science	English and Humanities	Natural Sciences, Mathematics, and Engineering	Business	Education
Background					
Sex	+	0	0	0	+
When chose occupation	0	0	+	0	0
Number years experience at current job	0	+	0	0	+
Worked in past, not now	−	0	−	0	0
Number years employed full time since graduation	+	0	0	+	0
Number graduate courses	0	0	0	−	0
Heavy industry employer	0	0	−	0	−
Education employer	−	0	−	0	−
Government employer	0	0	−	−	0
Married	+	0	+	0	0
Relationship					
College increased ability to think clearly	0	0	+	+	0
College taught knowledge and skills used in current job	0	0	0	+	+
Use content on major courses in current job	+	+	0	0	+
Work with colleagues trained in field	0	+	0	0	0
Use content of other undergraduate courses in job	+	0	0	+	0

*A plus sign means that the variable is significantly related to greater job satisfaction at the .05 level. A minus sign indicates a significant relationship to lower job satisfaction at the .05 level. Zero signifies no relationship. Variables in regression equation, but not significant: college grade-point average, selectivity of institution business firm employer, single, supervise people trained in same field, recommend major as preparation for current job, number of college-taught, work activities not performed in current job.

of major. But this is particularly true in economics and other social sciences, and education. The longer they have worked full time, the more satisfied they are with their job. If they are satisfied with their work, one would expect them to work as long as their job was secure. Moreover, as seniority is acquired, workers probably get more responsibility and more satisfying jobs. For economics and social science majors, lower job satisfaction is associated with having worked in the past but not currently working full time. That they are significantly less satisfied may be because they quit their last job precisely because they were dissatisfied with it. For economics and other social science majors, this relationship and the sex effect are the only two background concomitants that hold up in the final equation. Marital status and number of years of full-time work become insignificant when income is forced into the regression. Focusing on the relationship step (Table 5.1), it is apparent that these variables add little to the proportion of variance in explaining job satisfaction—2.5 percentage points. Only two relationship variables are important in explaining job satisfaction for economics and other social science majors, and only one remains significant in the final equation (Table 5.2).

Being employed by an educational institution is also associated with lower job satisfaction. This negative relationship may be a proxy for dissatisfaction with lower income and lower job level, since those who work in the education sector (few B.A. recipients are at the professorial level) typically earn less than their counterparts in other employment sectors and have less opportunity for advancement within the sector. When income and the job level variables enter the regression equation, the significant education-sector/job-satisfaction relationship no longer exists (Table 5.3). In fact, working in the education sector is no longer an important determinant of job satisfaction for all majors.

For respondents in this group of major fields, using the content of major courses in the current job is associated with greater satisfaction in that job, as is using the content of other undergraduate courses. However, only this last relationship holds up in the final analysis. It may be the use of other skills, in addition to those learned in major courses, which leads to promotion, and consequently, to greater satisfaction.

Income alone increases the explained variance by 2.1 percentage points (Table 5.1). The greater the income, the greater the job satisfaction. When other education-oriented variables were allowed to enter, only one entered as significant for the economics and other social science majors. Responding that the B.A. was necessary for promotion is associated with greater job satisfaction. This response could be a proxy for having a higher level position and therefore being more satisfied with status. However, this promotion variable remains significant even after allowing such job level variables as setting one's own hours, designing one's own work program, and having policymaking and decision-making responsibility to enter the regression equation.

TABLE 5.3

Important Variables Associated with Job Satisfaction in Final Step, by Major

Variable	Sign of Variable if Significant*				
	Economics and Social Science	English and Humanities	Natural Sciences, Mathematics, and Engineering	Business	Education
Background					
Sex	+	+	0	0	0
When chose occupation	0	0	+	0	0
Number years experience with current employer	0	0	0	0	+
Worked in past, not now	−	0	−	0	0
Number graduate courses	0	0	0	−	−
Heavy industry employer	0	+	−	0	0
Government employer	0	0	0	−	0
Single	0	0	+	0	0
Married	0	0	+	0	0
Relationship					
College taught knowledge and skills used in current job	0	0	0	0	+
Supervise people trained in field	0	0	0	−	0
Work with colleagues trained in field	0	+	0	0	0
Use content of other undergraduate courses in job	+	0	0	0	0
Income	+	+	+	+	0

Supervise people trained in field	0	0	0	−
Work with colleagues trained in field	0	+	0	0
Use content of other undergraduate courses in job	+	0	0	0
Income	+	+	+	+
Other education				
College taught skill which enabled me to get first job	0	0	+	0
College increased chance of finding a good job	0	0	+	0
College helped choose life goals	0	+	+	+
B.A. was factor in hiring	0	0	+	0
B.A. was necessary for promotion	+	0	0	0
Other job				
Can set own hours	0	0	0	+
Can design own work program	0	0	+	0
Have policy and decision-making responsibility	+	+	+	+
Am self-employed	+	0	0	0
Skills fully utilized	+	+	+	+

*Variables in regression equation, but not significant: college grade-point average, selectivity of institution, number of years employed full time since graduation, business firm employer, education employer, college increased ability to think clearly, use content of major courses, recommend major as preparation for current job, number of college-taught, work activities not performed in current job. A plus sign means that the variable is significantly related to greater job satisfaction at the .05 level. A minus sign indicates a significant relationship to lower job satisfaction at the .05 level. A zero signifies no relationship.

111

Two job-oriented variables, both signifying a sense of autonomy, are important in explaining job satisfaction for the economics and other social science majors. Together, having policymaking and decision-making responsibility and being self-employed increase the R^2 in explaining greater job satisfaction by 3.5 percentage points.

Along with feeling they have some autonomy on the job, greater satisfaction for working is also associated with the feeling that their skills are fully utilized. These skills probably include those learned in and outside of college. This variable, after controlling for all the background, relationship, income, and other education- and job-oriented variables, contributes by far the most variance in explaining job satisfaction (except for the background variables) for the economics and other social science majors (a 4.6 percentage point increase in the R^2 in Table 5.1).

English and Other Humanities Majors

The background variables explain 6.3 percent of the job satisfaction variance for the English and other humanities majors (Table 5.1). After the relationship step, only one variable is important in explaining greater satisfaction: the greater the number of years of experience in the current job. However, by the final step, this variable is insignificant, and two others are significantly related to greater satisfaction: being female and being employed in heavy industry.

Years of experience is probably a proxy for college having helped workers choose their life goals, since it is no longer significant when the life-goals variable enters the regression. Contrary to much current speculation, some humanities majors must have found jobs that fit in with their life goals. Those who had stayed in one job the longest were probably helped in selecting a career by college. Sex becomes a significant variable when the income and job level variables enter. Possibly, these aspects of the job are more highly valued by women humanities majors, or women were more willing to accept lower-paying jobs. It is only when the variable of skills fully utilized enters that being employed in heavy industry becomes significant. Unlike humanities majors employed in other sectors, those in heavy industry think that fully utilizing their skills is an important aspect of job satisfaction. Since heavy industry is probably the sector least related to the contents of humanities courses, humanists in this sector who think that their skills are fully utilized are almost certainly referring to a broader variety of skills than those acquired in college courses.

For English and other humanities majors, the relationship variables contribute 3.9 percentage points to the explained variance. Two of the variables are significantly related to greater job satisfaction: using the content of major courses in the current job and working with colleagues who are also trained in the humanities. Only the latter remained significant in the final step. When the skills fully utilized variable enters the regression, using the content of major courses drops to insignificance. Again, it is not so much the use of major that is important, but the use of work-related abilities that may have been acquired in or outside of college.

Even though higher earnings are significantly related to greater job satisfaction, the income variable increases the R^2 by a mere 0.6 percentage point in the regression by humanities majors. The one other education-oriented variable important to greater satisfaction is that college very much helped workers choose their life goals. The contribution to the explained variance in this case is 1.1 percentage points.

As in the regression for economics and other social science majors—and, in fact, in all regressions by major—having policymaking and decision-making responsibility in the job and feeling that skills are fully utilized are significantly related to greater job satisfaction.

Natural Science, Mathematics, and Engineering Majors

For natural science, mathematics, and engineering majors, the background variables explain 7.5 percent of the job satisfaction variance (Table 5.1). After the relationship step, six background variables are important concomitants of job satisfaction, two positively and four negatively.

Being married and having chosen their occupation more recently, rather than before or during college, are significantly associated with greater job satisfaction. The latter relationship is surprising, given that those using science or engineering in their jobs certainly had to prepare during college—that is, select their careers early. Perhaps these majors are most satisfied if they are not using their college-acquired training. In fact, among the relationship variables, use of courses is not significant. This finding—that greater satisfaction is associated with later career choice—could also indicate that science majors at the B.A. level are more satisfied in business than in science careers, in which the progress of the B.A. recipient is limited. Settings other than business tend to decrease the probable level of job satisfaction.

Neither years of experience nor years of full-time employment is important to job satisfaction for these majors. However, having worked in the past but not being currently employed full time is associated with lower satisfaction, as it was for the economics and other social science majors.

Three employment sectors—heavy industry, education, and government—as opposed to business and other sectors are related to lower job satisfaction for the natural science, mathematics, and engineering majors. But working in education and government becomes insignificant in the final equation. The education sector variable drops in importance when the income variable enters, indicating that dissatisfaction with a job in education means dissatisfaction with the lower pay in this sector. The government variable becomes insignificant when the skills fully utilized variable enters the equation. Dissatisfaction with a government job means dissatisfaction with the lack of opportunity to use skills optimally in this sector.

The relationship variables contribute 3.3 percentage points to the proportion of variance in explaining job satisfaction. Only one variable enters significantly and, by the final step, it loses its importance. At first, the response that college education very much increased the ability to think clearly was significantly related to greater job satisfaction, but in controlling for two autonomy and job-level variables, this relationship variable reduces to insignificance. For those who majored in the natural sciences, mathematics, and engineering, college may have taught a "scientific" way of thinking which these respondents may have translated into an ability to "think clearly."

Like the social science and humanities majors, these majors indicated that the more they earn, the more satisfied they are with their job. The income variable adds 3.3 percentage points to the explained variance.

The other education-oriented variables contribute 3.8 percentage points to the R^2. Sharing the importance, in relation to greater satisfaction, are college teaching a skill that enabled workers to get their first job, college increasing the chances of finding a good job, college helping workers choose their life goals, and the B.A. as a factor in being hired by their current employer. More than respondents in any other major field, it seems, these natural science, mathematics, and engineering majors are more likely to be satisfied if they see their baccalaureate degree performing a credentialing function. Those with satisfying jobs tend to credit their degree with helping secure the job. If screening is based on the type of degree, those with degrees in the sciences or engineering probably are favored.

The other job-oriented variables contribute an increment of 2.3 percentage points to the R^2. As in the other four regressions, having policymaking and decision-making responsibilities is significantly associated with greater job satisfaction. Another autonomy job level indicator, being able to design the individual work program, is significant in the same direction for natural science, mathematics, and engineering majors.

As in all other regressions by major, being able to fully utilize skills on the job is related to greater job satisfaction, even after controlling for all other variables (Table 5.3). The skills fully utilized variable alone accounts for 4.8 percentage points of the total explained variance.

Business Majors

For business majors, the background variables explain about 6.2 percent of the job satisfaction variance (Table 5.1). Only three variables are important after the relationship step. Like the economics and other social science majors, significantly related to greater job satisfaction is the number of years employed full time since graduation. Also, this variable is no longer significant in the final step. In both regressions, it is a proxy for earning a higher salary.

Significantly associated with lower satisfaction for business majors is having taken more graduate courses. Perhaps those who have taken more graduate work subsequently view themselves as overqualified for their jobs, or perhaps there is a discrepancy between what they planned for themselves and what the outcomes were. Also related to lower satisfaction is being employed in government, where business principles are less likely to be applied.

The relationship variables account for 3.6 percentage points of the variance in explaining job satisfaction. When they first enter, three variables—college increasing the ability to think clearly, college teaching knowledge and skills used in the current job, and using the content of undergraduate courses (other than major) in the current job—are significantly associated with greater job satisfaction. By the final step, all three are reduced to insignificance. The other education and job variables become more important.

For business majors, although the relationship variable, supervising people trained in their field, is insignificant after the relationship step, it becomes significantly associated with lower job satisfaction once salary is controlled for. Perhaps business majors feel more uncomfortable working with other business majors, even if they are in a supervisory position and earning more income; or perhaps, even in their supervisory position they are earning a lower salary than they expected. Supervising people in their field is significantly correlated with higher income ($r = .26$; $p \leq .01$). And, of course, higher income is significantly correlated with greater job satisfaction ($r = .22$; $p \leq .05$). Another possibility is that business majors are a rather homogeneous group who, when working together, feel they must be even more competitive to climb the ladder of success.

With the addition of income, the R^2 increases by 3.5 percentage points. Business majors, on the average, earn more than other majors, but they also have the greatest variance in salaries, as shown by the means and standard deviations in Table 5.4.

TABLE 5.4

Income Means and Standard Deviations, by Major

	Economics and Social Science	English and Humanities	Natural Sciences, Mathematics, and Engineering	Business	Education
Mean	$15,754	$12,253	$16,865	$19,353	$10,320
Standard Deviation	(7,997)	(6,520)	(7,009)	(9,085)	(3,800)

The other education-oriented variables contribute only 1.1 percentage points to the R^2, with only one variable important for business majors. Viewing college as having helped them choose their life goals is significantly related to greater job satisfaction for workers. Other job-related variables add 2.4 percentage points to the explained variance. Important here, in addition to having policymaking and decision-making responsibility, is designing the work program. A sense of autonomy and having a higher position are significant aspects of job satisfaction. For business majors, as for all others, thinking that they fully utilize their skills in their jobs significantly relates to greater job satisfaction and, in this case, increases the explained variance by 5.2 percentage points.

Education Majors

For the education majors, the background variables account for 6.4 percent of the variance in explaining job satisfaction. Being female and working more years at the current job are significantly and positively related to job satisfaction after the relationship step. But when the skills fully utilized variable enters, the sex variable becomes insignificant, probably indicating that sex differences in job satisfaction for education majors reflect male and female differences in feeling that skills are fully utilized. Women are more likely than men to think elementary and secondary school teaching provides an opportunity to fully utilize their skills.

Significantly related to lower job satisfaction are taking more graduate courses and being employed in the education sector. Again, this latter variable becomes insignificant with the addition of skills fully utilized. Women more than men who teach think they are using their skills.

The relationship variables for education majors account for 5.7 percentage points of the variance, the greatest increase of all categories of majors. The two most important variables reflect the predominance of women in this field. As in the regression by women (Chapter 4), college having taught knowledge and skills used in the current job and using the content of major courses in the job are significantly related to greater job satisfaction. However, as with other major fields, when the variable of skills fully utilized enters the regression, using the content of major courses becomes insignificant.

Contrary to the pattern in the other four regressions, income is not a significant concomitant of job satisfaction for these education majors.* Other education-oriented variables are not important in relation to job satisfaction,

---

*Not only do education majors have the lowest mean income of any group, but the variance in income for this group is also almost half as big as the next lowest group.

once the background and relationship variables are controlled. Education majors, most of whom expect to teach, enter their careers for other than financial reasons (Bisconti 1975).

In addition to policymaking and decision-making responsibility, however, setting their own hours is significantly associated with greater job satisfaction. For teachers this last variable probably differentiates between those who have a say about when their courses are taught and those who have no control over the schedule. Finally, as in the other regressions, fully utilizing their skills in the job is a very important facet of satisfaction with that job, in this case increasing the R^2 by 4.3 percentage points.

There is no one relationship variable that is consistently important across all five majors. Since the most popular definition of relationship is the match between the person's major and his job, and the most popular suggested cause of the college-educated worker's dissatisfaction with his job is the mismatch, one might hypothesize that the variable, using the content of major courses in the current job, would be a significant concomitant of job satisfaction. However, after the relationship step, this variable is significant in only three regressions: the three groups of majors currently having the most trouble finding "related" jobs. In the final analysis, after controlling for income, other education- and job-oriented variables, and skills fully utilized, using the content of major courses is not at all significant in any regression. Content seems to be representing factors introduced later in the analysis. It appears that factors other than relationship can substitute for it in helping to achieve job satisfaction.

INCOME

How important is the relationship of one's job to education in explaining differences in income within and across majors? Do some majors find that they earn more if they hold jobs more related to their college training (for example, business and engineering majors), while for others relationship has nothing to do with their salary?

Table 5.5 shows the five steps in these income regressions by major. The same variables were allowed to enter in the same way as in the job-satisfaction regressions, except, of course, that income is the dependent variable. As for the job-satisfaction regressions, the attempt was to determine the effect of relationship on income rather than to predict income.

Economics and Other Social Science Majors

The background variables explain 36 percent of the income variance for economics and other social science majors (Table 5.4). All variables entered

TABLE 5.5

R^2s in Income Regressions at Each Step, by Major

Variable	Economics and Social Science (N = 1,032)	English and Humanities (N = 730)	Natural Sciences, Mathematics, and Engineering (N = 1,049)	Business (N = 688)	Education (N = 456)
Background	.360	.366	.336	.215	.502
Relationship	.374	.378	.369	.252	.508
Other education variables	.385	.385	.379	.279	
Other job variables	.414	.399	.404	.397	.526
Skills fully used	–	–	–	–	.531

and remained significant, except for those indicating marital status and graduate courses, which did not enter as significant in any of the five regressions.

Since women earn significantly less than men, sex is significantly related to income in all regressions by major (Table 5.6). Controlling for sex differences, for economics and other social science majors, three background variables are significantly related to lower income: having chosen their occupation more recently (more than five years after graduation), having worked in the past but not currently working full time, and being employed in the education sector.

The probability of earning a higher salary is greatly enhanced by having a high college grade-point average, graduating from a high-selectivity institution, working for the current employer many years, and having worked at any job full time for many years since graduation. Also associated with higher income for economics and other social science majors is being employed by a business firm, heavy industry, or government.

Controlling for all background variables, the relationship variables add a mere 1.4 percentage points to the explanation of variance in income. Most important, for these majors, in explaining higher salaries are supervising people trained in their field and using the content of undergraduate courses in their current job. It is probably the "supervising" aspect of the first variable, rather than the "trained in their field" aspect which is significantly associated with higher earnings. When the variables indicating that college increased leadership ability and that workers can set their own hours enter the regression, supervising people trained in their field becomes insignificant.

That using the content of major courses is not related to income level, but that using the content of other undergraduate courses is, indicates that for most social science graduates promotion and salary increases are affected more

TABLE 5.6

Important Variables Associated with Income after Relationship Step, by Major

Variables	Sign of Variable if Significant*				
	Economics and Social Science	English and Humanities	Natural Sciences, Mathematics, and Engineering	Business	Education
Background					
Sex	–	–	–	–	–
Grade-point average	+	0	+	+	0
Selectivity of institution	+	+	+	+	+
When chose occupation	–	0	0	0	+
Number years experience with current employer	+	+	+	+	+
Worked in past, not now	–	–	0	0	0
Number years employed full time since graduation	+	+	+	+	+
Business firm employer	+	+	+	0	+
Heavy industry employer	+	+	+	0	+
Education employer	–	–	–	–	0
Government employer	+	+	0	0	+
Single	0	0	–	0	+
Married	0	+	–	0	+
Relationship					
College increased ability to think clearly	0	0	+	0	0
Use content of major course or job	0	0	–	0	0
Supervise people trained in field	+	+	+	+	0
Use content or other undergraduate courses in job	+	0	0	0	0
Number of work activities college prepared, but not doing	–	0	0	0	0

*A plus sign means that variable is significantly related to greater income at the .05 level. A minus sign indicates a significant relationship to lower income at the .05 level. A zero signifies no relationship. Variables in regression equation, but not significant: number of graduate courses, college taught knowledge and skills used in current job, work with colleagues trained in field, recommend preparation for current job.

by their full repertoire of skills than by how related their major is to work. Those who supplement their major with useful courses, and later use these, earn more. Also, significantly related to higher earnings is the fewer number of work activities college prepared workers to do that they are not doing, or the number of "useless" work activities. Higher salaries tend to be awarded to those economics and social science majors who more fully utilize all their college skills, implying that if less valuable nonmajor courses are taken but not used, the graduate will earn less.

The other education-oriented variables contribute an increment of 1.1 percentage points to the R^2. Two variables are significantly related to lower income—college teaching a skill to get the first job and college providing contacts which helped get the current job (Table 5.7). Related to higher income are college increasing leadership ability and chances of finding a good job. When college education functions in a more general sense, economics and other social science majors tend to earn higher salaries; when it operates only in a specific sense by providing entry-level skills or job-securing contacts, these majors tend to have lower-paying positions.

Increasing the proportion of variance explained by 2.9 percentage points are the other job-oriented variables. Two autonomy, higher-job-level indicators are significantly associated with higher earnings: setting own hours and having policymaking and decision-making responsibility. These are also prominent aspects of greater job satisfaction, even after controlling for level of income.

One of the most important aspects of job satisfaction, however, plays a negligible role in affecting salary level, if, indeed, it plays any role at all. Whether the respondents think their skills are fully utilized in the job has no relation to the amount of money they earn.

English and Other Humanities Majors

The background variables explain only slightly more of the variance in income for the English and other humanities majors (36.6 percent) than for the economics and other social science majors (36.0 percent). As in the other four regressions, being female is significantly associated with lower income. Also related are having worked in the past but not currently working full time and being employed in the education sector. When the job-oriented variable of setting individual hours enters the regression, the education sector variable becomes insignificant. Probably, when a humanities major becomes an administrator or reaches some job position above teacher status in which his hours are more flexible, his salary is greater.

After the relationship step, when workers choose their occupation is not significant; the earlier they choose it becomes significantly related to higher income when the education-oriented variable—college teaching a skill to get the first job—enters the regression. For those who believe their college education helped them secure their first job, higher earnings are associated with having chosen to prepare for their occupation before or during college rather than sometime after graduation.

As in the other regressions by major, higher selectivity of the institution, the number of years of experience with their current employer, and the number of years employed full time are significantly associated with higher earnings. Also, important for the humanities majors are being married and being employed in business, heavy industry, or government.

The relationship variables give an increment of only 1.2 percentage points to the model for explaining income differences (Table 5.5). Only one relationship variable is significantly associated with higher income for the humanities majors: supervising people trained in their field of study. Since this variable is no longer significant when having policymaking and decision-making responsibility is controlled for, it is the supervising aspect rather than the relationship aspect that is important in explaining greater earnings. Relationship, for English and other humanities majors, really has no effect.

The other education-oriented variables add only .7 percentage point to the R^2. Two are significantly associated with higher salaries—college teaching a skill for the first job and increasing chances of finding a good job. The other job-oriented variables contribute 1.4 percentage points to the R^2. Two are also important in explaining higher salaries: setting own hours and having policymaking and decision-making responsibility. Both indicate a certain amount of autonomy in the job and a higher level position. As for economics and other social science majors, thinking their skills are fully utilized has no effect on reported income level or vice versa.

Natural Science, Mathematics, and Engineering Majors

For the natural science, mathematics, and engineering majors, the background variables account for 33.6 percent of the variance in explaining income differences. In addition to being female, other variables significantly associated with lower salaries are being employed in the education sector, and being single or married rather than divorced, separated, or widowed. This is the only group of majors in which being married is a negative concomitant with income level.

In addition to high institutional selectivity, more years of experience with current employer, and working full time, important to high earnings are higher college grade-point average and being employed in business or heavy industry rather than government, education, or some other sector. All these significant background variables remain significant, even after controlling for relationship and other education- and job-oriented aspects.

TABLE 5.7

Important Variables Associated with Income
in Final Step, by Major

	Sign of Variable if Significant*				
Variable	Economics and Social Science	English and Humanities	Natural Sciences, Mathematics, and Engineering	Business	Education
Background					
Sex	–	–	–	–	–
Grade-point average	+	0	+	+	0
Selectivity of institution	+	+	+	+	+
When chose occupation	–	–	0	0	0
Number years experience at current job	+	+	+	+	0
Worked in past, not now	–	–	0	0	0
Number years employed full time since graduation	+	+	+	+	+
Business firm employer	+	+	+	0	+
Heavy industry employer	+	+	+	0	+
Education employer	–	0	–	–	0
Government employer	+	+	0	0	+
Single	0	0	–	0	+
Married	0	+	–	+	+
Relationship					
College increased ability to think clearly	0	0	+	+	0
Use content of major courses in job	0	0	–	0	0

	Sign of Variable if Significant*				
Variable	Economics and Social Science	English and Humanities	Natural Sciences, Mathematics, and Engineering	Business	Education
Supervise people trained in field	0	0	+	+	0
Use content of other undergraduate courses in field	+	0	0	0	0
Number of work activities prepared, but not doing	–	0	0	0	0
Other education					
College taught skill that enabled me to get first job	–	+	0	0	0
College increased leadership ability	+	0	0	0	0
College increased chances of finding a good job	+	+	+	0	0
College provided contacts which helped get current job	–	0	0	0	0
Other job					
Can set own hours	+	+	+	+	0
Have policymaking and decision-making responsibility	+	+	+	+	+
Am self-employed	0	0	+	+	0
Skills fully utilized	0	0	0	0	+

*A plus sign means that the variable is significantly related to greater income at the .05 level. A minus sign indicates a significant relationship to lower income at the .05 level. A zero signifies no relationship. Variables in regression equation, but not significant: number of graduate courses, college taught knowledge and skills used in current job, work with colleagues trained in field, recommend major as preparation for current job, B.A. was a factor in being hired.

The relationship variables increase the proportion of explained income variance by 3.3 percentage points. Significantly related to greater income are college having increased the ability to think clearly and supervising people trained in the same field. Contrary to humanities majors, the relationship aspect of this latter variable holds up for the natural science, mathematics, and engineering majors. Using the content of their major courses on the job is significantly related to lower income, even after controlling for the variables indicating position level or job status (Table 5.7). Considering the other two significant relationship variables, apparently these majors view the more general rather than specific facets of their college education as more useful in climbing the income ladder.

The other education-oriented variables give a 1 percent increment to the R^2, due to the positive significance of college increasing their chances of finding a good job. Adding 2.5 percentage points to the R^2, three other job-oriented variables—setting own hours, having policymaking and decision-making responsibility, and being self-employed—are significantly associated with higher earnings. Again, autonomy and job level are important in explaining differences in income.

Business Majors

Compared with other categories of majors, the background variables for business majors contribute the least variance (21.5 percentage points) to the explanation of income differences. Four variables are significant in all regressions by major—sex, selectivity of institution, number of years of experience with current employer, and number of years employed full time since graduation. In addition, higher college grade-point average is significantly related to higher salaries for business majors, while being employed in the education sector is related to lower salaries. Once the job variable indicating self-employment enters, being married becomes significantly related to higher earnings.

The relationship variables account for 3.7 percentage points of the variance in explaining income differences for business majors. Significantly related to higher income is supervising people trained in the same field. As in the regression of natural science, mathematics, and engineering majors, this variable remains significant after controlling for job level. However, as with economics and other social science majors, the greater the number of work activities that college prepared them to do but which they do not do ("useless activities"), the lower their reported salaries. General college education rather than specific skills taught seem to contribute to higher earning power. Those who learned skills which are useful later, rather than gaining less relevant skills in college, earn more. When the variable indicating self-employment enters, the "useless" variable becomes insignificant. It is when the business major is a business owner that he explicitly uses the work skills learned in college. When the self-employed variable enters, the relationship variable—college increasing ability to think clearly—becomes significant. The business owner, then, values not only the specific skills learned in college, but also the more general way of thinking.

Although other education-oriented variables add 2.7 percentage points to the R^2, none entering the regression remained significant in the final equation. A rather large increment in the R^2 (11.8 percentage points) is due to the addition of three job-oriented variables, the same three that entered for the natural science, mathematics, and engineering majors: setting own hours, policymaking and decision-making responsibility, and being self-employed.

Education Majors

The greatest proportion of the variance accounted for by the background variables (50.2 percent) is given in the regression for education majors. In addition to the four variables significant in all five regressions, significantly associated with higher income are the more recently workers chose their occupation, being employed by a business firm, heavy industry, or government, and being single or married (Table 5.6). Once their job level is controlled for, however, when workers chose their occupation and the number of years of experience with their current employer become unimportant in explaining income differences.

For education majors, the relationship of college education to work is even less important than for the other majors, whether it is considered in the general or specific sense. No relationship variable is significant in explaining income differences. Neither are the other education-oriented variables important to education majors, even controlling for the employment sector.

Contributing 1.8 percentage points to the explained variance is the one job-oriented variable significantly related to higher salaries: having policymaking and decision-making responsibility. Unlike other majors, however, the view of education majors that their skills are being fully utilized in their job is significantly related to higher earnings. This variable increases the R^2 by .5 percentage point.

Relationship has little if any effect on income level. If the college-educated worker views his education as useful in his job or as instrumental in increasing his salary, it is probably the more general rather than the specific abilities acquired in college that he considers. Regardless of major, what is more important in association with earning power are the respondent's sex, the selectivity of his undergraduate institution, the number of years he has been employed full time since graduation, and having policymaking and decision-making responsibility in his job. Substantial differences are revealed among the various majors when considering such variables as employment sector, grade-point average, and other education- and job-oriented dimensions.

6

THE RELATIONSHIP OF
COLLEGE TO CAREER
OUTCOMES BY OCCUPATION

Just as there were differences among groups of majors in explaining job satisfaction and income, so there are differences among the five groups of occupations.

The largest generic occupational category is accounting, administration, and sales, with 1,174 cases, which includes accounting, financial analysis, business and government administration, business ownership, buying, purchasing, sales, and brokerage. The next largest is education, with 1,052 cases, which includes education administration, elementary and secondary teaching, and professorial positions. The mathematics, science, and engineering category (546 cases) includes computer science and programming, systems analysis, mathematics, statistics, actuarial positions, biological, physical, and natural sciences, and engineering. The two smallest generic occupational categories are allied health and social service (263 cases)—which include allied health work, hygiene, lab technology, therapy, dietary positions, nursing, pharmacy, counseling; social science, social welfare, and community work; and office work (268) cases incorporating administrative assistance, middle-level office work, and secretarial and clerical positions.

JOB SATISFACTION

The variables for the job satisfaction regressions by occupation were forced in the same six steps as those in the regressions by major. Therefore, Table 6.1 is comparable to Table 5.1. Most other tables are also comparable.

Mathematics, Science, and Engineering Occupations

The background variables account for 7.2 percentage points of the variance in explaining job satisfaction for those in mathematics, science, and engineering occupations (Table 6.1). Important to greater job satisfaction are being female rather than male and being married rather than single, separated, divorced, or widowed (Table 6.2). Significantly associated with lower satisfaction are having worked in the past but not currently working full time and being employed in heavy industry or education. However, by the final step these employment sector variables are insignificant (Table 6.3). Because the education sector variable is no longer significant when salary enters the regression, the respondents in education seem to equate job dissatisfaction with dissatisfaction with low pay. But for those in heavy industry, feeling that their skills are fully utilized in their job causes this employment sector variable to become insignificant. In this case, dissatisfaction with work means dissatisfaction with poor chances of using all skills.

The relationship variables for those in mathematics, science, and engineering contribute only 2 percentage points to the proportion of explained variance, and only one variable is significantly related to greater job satisfaction: college having taught the knowledge and skills used in the current job. When the other education-oriented variables enter, however, especially college increasing the chances of finding a good job and helping with the choice of life goals, the relationship variable loses its significance. This result probably indicates that respondents who gained most from more general career-related

TABLE 6.1

R²s in Job Satisfaction Regressions at Each Step, by Occupation

Step	Mathematics, Science, and Engineering (N = 546)	Office Work (N = 268)	Accounting, Administration, and Sales (N = 1,174)	Allied Health and Social Service (N = 263)	Education (N = 1052)
Background	.072	.105	.059	.118	.034
Relationship	.092	.171	.076	.179	.076
Income	.127	.187	.096	.187	.076
Other education variables	.159	.219	.099	–	.107
Other job variables	.187	–	.132	.203	.125
Skills fully used	.241	.260	.183	.259	.187

TABLE 6.2

Important Variables Associated with Job Satisfaction after Relationship Step, by Occupation

Variable	Sign of Variable if Significant*				
	Mathematics, Science, and Engineering	Office Work	Accounting, Administration, and Sales	Allied Health and Social Service	Education
Background					
Sex	+	0	+	0	+
Number years experience with current employment	0	0	+	0	+
Worked in past, not now	−	0	−	−	0
Number years employed full time since graduation	0	0	+	0	0
Number graduate courses	0	0	0	+	0
Heavy industry employer	−	+	0	0	0
Education employer	−	0	0	0	0
Single	0	−	0	0	0
Married	+	0	0	0	0
Relationship					
College increased ability to think clearly	0	0	+	0	0
College taught knowledge and skills used in current job	+	0	+	0	+
Use content of major courses in job	0	0	0	+	+
Colleagues trained in field	0	0	0	0	+
Use content of other undergraduate courses in job	0	+	0	0	0

*A plus sign means that the variable is significantly related to greater job satisfaction at the .05 level. A minus sign indicates a significant relationship to lower job satisfaction at the .05 level. A zero signifies no relationship. Variables in regression equation, but not significant: college grade-point average, selectivity of institution, when chose occupation, business firm employer, government employer, supervise people in same field, recommend major as preparation for current job, number of college-taught work activities not performed in current job.

TABLE 6.3

Important Variables Associated with Job Satisfaction in Final Step, by Occupation

	Sign of Variable if Significant*				
Variable	Mathematics, Science, and Engineering	Office Work	Accounting, Administration, and Sales	Allied Health and Social Service	Education
Background					
Sex	+	+	+	0	0
Number years experience with current employer	0	0	+	0	+
Worked in past, not now	–	0	–	–	0
Married	+	0	0	0	0
Relationship					
College taught knowledge and skills used in current job	0	0	+	0	+
Use content of major courses in job	0	0	0	+	0
Colleagues trained in field	0	0	0	0	+
Use content of other undergraduate courses in job	0	+	0	0	0

Income	+	+	0	0
Other education				
College increased leadership ability	0	0	+	+
College increased chances of finding a good job	+	+	0	+
College taught skills that enabled me to get first job	0	0	0	−
College helped choose life goals	+	0	0	0
B.A. was necessary for promotion	+	0	0	0
Other job				
Can design own work program	+	0	+	0
Have policymaking and decision-making responsibility	0	0	+	0
Am self-employed	0	0	+	0
Skills fully utilized	+	+	+	+

*A plus sign means that the variable is significantly related to greater job satisfaction at the .05 level. A minus sign indicates a significant relationship to lower job satisfaction at the .05 level. A zero signifies no relationship. Variables in regression equation, but not significant: college grade-point average, selectivity of institution, when chose occupation, number of years employed full time since graduation, number of graduate courses, business firm employer, heavy industry employer, education employer, government employer, single, college increased ability to think clearly, supervise people in same field, recommend major as preparation for current job, number of college-taught, work activities not performed, can set own hours.

aspects of their college education and not necessarily from specific skill training earn more.

Income adds a substantial 3.5 percentage points to the variance in explaining job satisfaction for these occupations. The greater the earnings, the greater the satisfaction. The set of other education-oriented variables contributes 3.2 percentage points to the explained variance. Three of them are significantly associated with greater job satisfaction: college increasing chances of finding a good job and the B.A. being necessary for promotion, and college helping with the choice of life goals. The first two may indicate the credentialing effect of the baccalaureate degree, although possibly those who feel they have good jobs and have been promoted are more satisfied. Part of their success is being credited to the credential. Similarly, if the job is consistent with life goals, satisfaction results, partially to the credit of the college experience.

Only one other job-oriented variable is significantly related to greater job satisfaction, increasing the R^2 by 2.8 percentage points. That the respondents in mathematics, science, and engineering are able to design their own work program and have a sense of autonomy in their job contributes substantially to their satisfaction. So too does the feeling that their skills are fully utilized; this variable alone increases the proportion of variance explained by 5.4 percentage points.

Office Work Occupations

Although the background variables account for 10.5 percentage points of the explained job satisfaction variance for office work occupations, only two variables are significant after the relationship step. Being employed in heavy industry is significantly associated with greater satisfaction, whereas being single is related to lower job satisfaction. However, when salary enters the regression, both variables become insignificant. Once salary and college increasing chances of a good job are controlled for, being female is significantly related to greater job satisfaction.

The relationship variables add 6.6 percentage points to the proportion of explained variance, with only one variable significant. For office workers, using the content of their undergraduate courses (other than major) in their job is concomitant with greater job satisfaction. Most likely, these courses are more vocational in type (for example, stenography, typing, accounting).

As in the regression by mathematics, science, and engineering occupations, higher earnings are significantly related to greater job satisfaction for office workers. The income variable contributes 1.6 percentage points to the explained variance. No other job-oriented variable and only one education-oriented variable, which increases the R^2 by 3.2 percentage points, is significantly associated with greater job satisfaction: college increasing chances of a good job. Even though few office workers perceive that their job is high level—only 36 percent say they have policymaking and decision-making responsibility—some have found satisfying jobs that they say are "good." More important, if they think their skills are fully utilized in the job, workers tend to express greater job satisfaction. The skills fully utilized variable accounts for 4.1 percent of the 26 percentage points of explained variance.

Accounting, Administration, and Sales Occupations

For accounting, administration, and sales, background variables contribute 5.9 percentage points to the proportion of variance in explaining job satisfaction, whereas being female, having been employed by the current employer many years, and having been employed many years full time are significantly related to greater job satisfaction, having worked in the past but not currently working full time is, surprisingly, associated with lower satisfaction. When income and college increasing leadership ability enter the regression, however, the number of years of full-time work becomes insignificant. Apparently, this variance acts as a proxy for higher salaries and job level.

The relationship variables increase the R^2 by 1.7 percentage points. Two variables—college increasing ability to think clearly and college teaching knowledge and skills used in the current job—are significantly related to greater job satisfaction. But once skills fully utilized enters the regression, the ability to think clearly variable becomes insignificant.

Income contributes 2 percentage points to the explained job satisfaction variance; as in the regressions by office work and mathematics, science, and engineering occupations, the higher the salary, the greater the satisfaction. The only other education-oriented variables significantly related to greater job satisfaction are being able to design the work program, having policymaking and decision-making responsibility, and being self-employed. All indicate greater autonomy in the job and higher job level. Of course, as in the other four regressions, feeling that skills are fully utilized significantly relates to greater satisfaction, adding an increment of 5.1 percentage points to the R^2.

Allied Health and Social Service Occupations

The background variables account for 11.8 percentage points of the variance in explaining job satisfaction for the allied health and social service occupations. Significantly related to lower satisfaction is having worked in the past but not currently working full time. Related to greater satisfaction is the greater number of graduate courses taken. This is the only occupation regression in which graduate courses have been important. When the job-oriented variable, designing the work program, enters the regression, however, the graduate-courses variable becomes insignificant. Perhaps employers promoted the workers partly because of their continued education so it is the higher status that contributes to greater satisfaction.

For the allied health and social service workers, the relationship variables account for 6.1 percentage points of the explained variance. Only one relationship variable is significant: using the content of major courses in the job. The more frequently workers use the content of their major, the greater their job satisfaction.

Unlike the first three occupational groups, income is not a factor in job satisfaction. Neither are the other education- and job-oriented variables. Skills fully utilized, however, increases the R^2 by 5.6 percentage points. Evidently, for allied health and social service workers, it is important to think they are fully utilizing their skills, especially those that were college prepared, in their work.

Education Occupations

For education, the background variables explain only 3.4 percent of the differences in job satisfaction. Being female and having more years of experience with the current employer are significantly associated with greater satisfaction. However, when the education-oriented variable, college increasing the chances of finding a good job, enters the regression, the sex variable becomes insignificant. Apparently, men more than women in education think their college education helped them find a good, satisfying job.

The relationship variables contribute 4.2 percentage points to the proportion of variance explaining job satisfaction. Three of these variables are significantly related to greater satisfaction: college teaching knowledge and skills used in the current job, using the content of major courses, and working with colleagues who were trained in the same field. When the skills fully utilized variable enters, using the content of the major becomes insignificant. Again, the skills referred to are those learned during the course of major study and beyond.

As in the allied health and social service regression, income is not a significant concomitant of job satisfaction for education occupations. The other education-oriented variables, however, account for 3.1 percentage points of the variance. Related to greater satisfaction are college increasing leadership ability and chances of finding a good job. But significantly associated with lower job satisfaction is college teaching a skill that enabled workers to get their first job. Increasing the R^2 by 1.8 percentage points is the one job-oriented variable significantly related to greater satisfaction: having policymaking and decision-making responsibility. As in all other occupational regressions, the skills fully utilized variable is significant for the education occupations.

Relationship is not a substantial factor in explaining job satisfaction for any of these occupational categories. Using the content of the major courses in the job is significant, in the final step, in only one case: in the regression by allied health and social service occupations. Only one variable, not a relationship variable, is significantly associated with job satisfaction across all occupations. As in the analysis by majors, the relationship between job satisfaction and feeling that skills are fully utilized is consistently significant across all occupations.

INCOME

The income regressions by occupation are comparable to those by major. First, the background and relationship variables were forced in; then the other education- and job-oriented variables were allowed to enter if significant at the .05 level.

Mathematics, Science, and Engineering Occupations

For mathematics, science, and engineering, the background variables account for 30.7 percentage points of the variance in explaining income differences (Table 6.4). Consistently significant across all occupations is the sex variable. Regardless of occupation, men earn more than women, even after controlling for job-level variables (Tables 6.5 and 6.6). Also significantly associated with higher incomes, for mathematics, science, and engineering, are higher college grade-point average, higher selectivity of undergraduate institution, more years of experience with the current employer and working full time since graduation, and the more graduate courses taken.

Significantly related to lower incomes are having chosen the occupation more recently rather than before or during college, having worked in the past but not working now, and being employed in the education sector.

Increasing the R^2 by 5.5 percentage points are the relationship variables. Those who use the content of their major in the job actually tend to have lower incomes, whereas those who supervise people trained in their field tend to have higher incomes (even controlling for the job-level variables).

The other education-oriented variables add 2.3 percentage points to the variance in explaining income differences. Lower salaries are associated with the response that college increases general knowledge, while higher salaries are significantly related to the statement that college increases chances of finding

TABLE 6.4

R^2s in Income Regressions at Each Step, by Occupation

Step	Mathematics, Science, and Engineering (N = 546)	Office Work (N = 268)	Accounting, Administration, and Sales (N = 1,174)	Allied Health and Social Service (N = 263)	Education (N = 1,052)
Background	.307	.555	.167	.442	.414
Relationship	.362	.586	.186	.456	.425
Other educa- tion variables	.385	—	.199	.474	.434
Other job variables	.420	.598	.250	.550	.446
Skills fully used	—	—	—	—	—

a good job. Evidently, for these occupations, the more specific rather than general college-taught abilities lead to good and higher paying jobs.

Increasing the R^2 by 3.5 percentage points are two other job-oriented variables. For mathematics, science, and engineering, being able to design work program and having policymaking and decision-making responsibility are significantly associated with higher earnings. In none of the five occupational regressions is the skills fully utilized variable a factor in explaining income differences.

Office Work Occupations

The background variables account for 55.5 percentage points of the variance for office work occupations, the largest proportion accounted for by the background variables in any occupational regression. With the three variables significant in all five regressions—sex, having worked in the past but not now, and the years employed full time since graduation—four other variables are significantly related to income. Office workers tend to report higher incomes if they graduated from a higher selectivity institution and are employed by business, heavy industry, and government.

Increasing the R^2 by 3.1 percentage points is one relationship variable: using the content of the major courses in the job. This probably shows that, although they may not have needed their college-taught abilities to get their current job, if workers used such knowledge and skills, they were more likely to be rewarded monetarily.

TABLE 6.5

Important Variables Associated with Income after Relationship Step, by Occupation

Variable	Sign of Variable if Significant*				
	Mathematics, Science, and Engineering	Office Work	Accounting Administration, and Sales	Allied Health and Social Service	Education
Background					
Sex	–	–	–	–	–
Grade-point average	+	0	+	0	0
Selectivity of institution	+	+	+	0	+
When chose occupation	–	0	–	0	+
Number of years experience with current employer	+	0	+	0	+
Worked in past, not now	–	–	–	–	–
Number years employed full time since graduation	+	+	+	+	+
Number graduate courses	+	0	0	0	+
Business firm employer	0	+	0	+	+
Heavy industry employer	0	+	0	+	0
Education employer	–	0	0	0	0
Government employer	0	+	0	0	0
Relationship					
Use content of major courses in job	–	+	–	0	0
Supervise people trained in field	+	0	+	0	+
Recommend major as preparation for job	0	0	+	0	0
Number work activities college prepared, but not doing	0	0	–	0	–

*A plus sign means that the variable is significantly related to greater income at the .05 level. A minus sign indicates a significant relationship to lower income at the .05 level. A zero signifies no relationship. Variables in regression equation, but not significant: single, married, college increased ability to think clearly, college taught knowledge and skills used in current job, work with colleagues trained in field, use content of other undergraduate courses in current job.

TABLE 6.6

Important Variables Associated with Income in Final Step, by Occupation

Variable	Sign of Variable if Significant[*]				
	Mathematics, Science, and Engineering	Office Work	Accounting, Administration, and Sales	Allied Health and Social Service	Education
Background					
Sex	−	−	−	−	−
Grade-point average	+	0	+	0	0
Selectivity of institution	+	+	+	0	+
When chose occupation	−	0	−	0	0
Number years experience with current employer	+	0	+	0	+
Worked in past, not now	−	−	−	−	−
Number years employed full time since graduation	+	+	+	+	+
Number graduate courses	+	0	0	0	+
Business firm employer	0	+	0	+	+
Heavy industry employer	0	+	0	+	0
Education employer	−	0	0	0	0
Government employer	0	+	ɔ	0	0

Relationship					
Use content of major courses in job	0	0	+	-	0
Supervise people trained in field	+	+	0	+	+
Recommend major as preparation for job	0	0	0	0	0
Number work activities college prepared but not doing	0	0	0	0	-
Other education					
College increased general knowledge	0	0	0	-	0
College taught skill that enabled me to get first job	0	-	0	0	0
College increased chances of finding a good job	0	+	0	+	0
B.A. was a factor in hiring	0	0	0	0	+
B.A. was necessary for promotion	+	0	0	0	0
College provided contacts that helped get current job	+	0	0	0	-
Other job					
Can set own hours	0	+	0	0	+
Can design own work program	0	0	0	+	0
Have policymaking and decision-making responsibility	+	+	+	+	+
Am self-employed	+	+	0	0	0
Skills fully utilized	0	0	0	0	0

*A plus sign means that the variable is significantly related to greater income at the .05 level. A minus sign indicates a significant relationship to lower income at the .05 level. A zero signifies no relationship. Variables in regression equation, but not significant: single, married, college increased ability to think clearly, college taught knowledge and skills used in current job, work with colleagues trained in field, use content of other undergraduate courses in current job.

For office work occupations, no other education-oriented and only one job-oriented variable significantly adds to the variance in explaining income. Those office workers who are self-employed report higher earnings; however, only 2 percent are self-employed.

Accounting, Administration, and Sales Occupations

The background variables account for the lowest proportion of explained variance for accounting, administration, and sales occupations: 16.7 percentage points. This occupational category also has the highest mean annual salary ($20,696 compared with $17,401 for mathematics, science, and engineering; $11,812 for allied health and social service, $11,597 for office work, and $10,193 for education). In addition to the three variables significant for all occupational groups, related to higher earnings are higher grade-point average, higher institutional selectivity, and more years of experience with current employer. Associated with lower earnings is having chosen the occupation more recently.

The relationship variables contribute 1.9 percentage points to the proportion of explained income variance. Those in accounting, administration, and sales occupations who state they supervise people in their field and who recommend their major as preparation for their job tend also to report higher salaries. But those who use the content of their major courses in the job and those to whom college gave fewer unused work skills ("useless activities") tend to earn less. These last two variables, however, become insignificant with the addition of the job-level variables.

Increasing the R^2 by 1.3 percentage points are the other education-oriented variables. Significantly related to lower income is college teaching a skill for the first job, whereas significantly associated with greater income is college increasing the chances of finding a good job. Those whose education emphasized general rather than specific skills tend to find jobs that pay more. The other job-oriented variables contribute a much greater proportion (5.1 percentage points) to the explained variance than the education-oriented variables. Three variables significantly related to higher earnings are setting own work hours, policymaking and decision-making responsibility, and self-employment.

Allied Health and Social Service Occupations

For the allied health and social service occupations, the background variables account for 44.2 percentage points of the variance in explaining income. In addition to the three variables significant in all five regressions, only two other background variables are significant. Those who work in business and heavy industry tend to report greater income than those in education, government, or any other sector.

This is the only occupational group for which the relationship variables have no effect: no relationship variable is significantly associated with income.

The other education-oriented variables increase the R^2 by 1.8 percentage points, with two significantly associated with greater income: responding that the B.A. is necessary for promotion and that college provides contacts that helped get the current job. For these occupations college was instrumental in helping workers attain higher incomes, not so much by content preparation but by credentialing effect and by provision of job-market contacts. Only one other job-oriented variable accounts for 7.6 percentage points of the explained variance. Those self-employed in the allied health and social service fields tend to earn more than those who work for others.

Education Occupations

The background variables for those in education occupations account for 41.4 percentage points of the variance in explaining income differences. Significantly related to higher incomes are the higher selectivity of the undergraduate institution, the more recent choice of occupation, the more years of experience with the current employer (tenure), the more graduate courses taken, and being employed by a business firm, along with the three background variables significant in all occupational regressions. When workers chose their occupation, however, becomes insignificant with the entrance of policymaking and decision-making responsibility. Evidently, those who are pulled into education occupations later in their work life are pulled into higher-level positions.

Contributing only 1.1 percentage points to the R^2 are the relationship variables. Related to greater income is supervising people trained in the same field, while related to lower income is more "useless activities."

Only 0.9 percentage points of the variance are accounted for by the other education-oriented variables, but two are significantly associated with income level. Related to greater earnings is the statement that the B.A. was a factor in being hired. Concomitant with lower income is responding that college provided contacts that helped get the current job. The other job-oriented variables contribute 1.2 percentage points to the proportion of explained variance, with two being significantly related to higher salaries: setting hours and having policymaking and decision-making responsibility.

In this analysis of income differences by occupational group, the set of background variables contributes the most of all five sets of variables (Table 6.4) to the explanation of income variance. Three background variables are consistently significant, in the same direction, in all five regressions: sex (higher income is associated more with men than with women), having worked in the past but not currently working full time (related to lower salaries), and the number of years of full-time employment since graduation (the more years of full-time work, the greater the income).

The relationship variables do not contribute much to understanding income differences. Not one variable is consistently significant across all occupations. The same condition holds for the sets of other education- and job-oriented variables. A variable first seen as important in job satisfaction—skills fully utilized—is not at all important in understanding salary levels. One can question the economists' assumption that more highly educated people who use their skills are more productive, and hence earn more.

7

THE MEANING OF A GOOD JOB

As discussed in Chapter 2, unrest is growing among educational researchers and policymakers over the general efficacy of the current system of higher education. Educational purposes and goals are being widely questioned. Much impressionistic writing points to the declining monetary value of obtaining a college degree: A graduate can no longer be sure of using his skills on a good job.

Some critics notwithstanding, there are many purposes to higher education, far more than merely providing students with specific skills for jobs. Indeed, college preparation for work includes the ability to think, read, write, calculate, learn, and get along with people. It also includes the ability to use nonworking hours constructively, either in complementing or substituting for the satisfaction that comes from work itself.

That the purpose of college is to enable graduates to get a "good job" has been the premise upon which much criticism of higher education has been based. Yet, there is no general agreement on what a "good job" is. What might be an undesirable job to intellectuals critiquing higher education might be a desirable position to one holding or seeking it.

This lack of clarity has resulted partly from lack of data. The findings of this study, which challenge some of the more destructive predictions presently in vogue, are based on a national survey of college graduates rather than on subjective views. Because first jobs are often temporary—indeed, half the graduates change career plans after college—the individuals surveyed were men and women who entered college in 1961. While the responses of the 4,000 baccalaureates now employed do not reveal the extent of unemployment nor the monetary payoff to college compared with different levels of education, they do indicate the benefits people derive from their college education, what they seek from their work, and what gives college-educated persons job satisfaction.

The most discussed purpose of education—to prepare people for the world of work—is easier to state than to define. The obvious aspect is learning specific skills, facts, processes, and knowledge that will be used directly in a job. Certain job skills are considered vocational, such as the ability to install plumbing. This training is thought by some to be undesirable, outside the purview of higher education, or an attempt by certain social elements to keep "lower-class people" in their substandard position.

Many universities are passive about the types of subjects that can be taught and directly applied in future jobs. For example, one school of thought maintains that students should be allowed to study what they will, and there should be enough jobs available so they can use their knowledge later in work. The question becomes, is it the role of education to train people who are "needed" by the labor market, or is it the obligation of the labor market to provide positions for all those who are trained? Some observers maintain that certain subjects are more "vocationally oriented" than others: That is, people can go into chemistry and be justified in assuming that a job as a chemist will be available upon graduation. However, those who study Latin may be less justified in assuming that they will be able to use their training in a future job.

All these expectations, of course, are too simplified. Vocational-oriented subjects are often defined too narrowly and other subjects are thrown out as vocationally irrelevant. It is unrealistic to expect all chemistry graduates to conduct chemical experiments in a laboratory. Often they do not end up conducting experiments, not only because these jobs are unavailable, but also because they would rather do something else, such as sell pharmaceuticals. It is also unrealistic to assume that the chemistry major who sells pharmaceuticals is not using his training.

Traditionally, the humanities have been considered one area in which graduates should not expect to find jobs that use their training. Yet, communications skills—writing, reading comprehension, and the like—are crucial in many jobs.

Baccalaureate graduates now in the labor force were asked what they would recommend as the most useful course for someone preparing for a job like theirs. Of the workers, 32 percent recommended psychology, 31 percent business administration, and 30 percent English—that nonvocational subject not generally considered useful in the job market. Since opportunities for jobs related to the major may not be available at graduation, colleges should focus on courses that teach students how to read, write, compute, learn, and work with people rather than how to do a specific chemistry experiment.

Also, a prime function of today's colleges should be to provide career information to students, before they enter college, when they are deciding whether to attend and what field to study, and all the way to the end, when they are making postcollege career plans. Colleges should indicate which jobs are available and stress that good jobs, or related jobs, just might not be available. It is a cop-out to argue, as some critics do, that college-trained youth expect "good jobs" and that the universities are failing because these jobs are unavailable. Colleges and universities must help students redefine the concept of "good jobs" and break down the expectation that a college education is merely a ticket to whatever job a student desires.

LIFE ENRICHMENT

An important question today is whether the role of postsecondary education is to provide a means to a good job or a way to a good life. There is vast literature on the impact of college on aspects of personal growth. College significantly affects life goals, social responsibility, family practices, ability to use leisure time, and the like. Indeed, in addition to their role in enriching jobs, colleges and universities should question their ability to help people enrich their nonworking lives. This study has indicated that, regardless of field, over 68 percent of the workers think their college education increased their general knowledge, about 35 percent believe it increased their ability to think clearly, over 20 percent think it increased their leadership ability, and another 20 percent think it helped them choose their life goals.

Education's critics should also be aware that, although 54 percent of the men and 36 percent of the women in a group of college freshmen in 1974 considered it important to be well off financially, approximately 60 percent thought it important to develop a philosophy of life, over 50 percent thought it important to raise a family, and over 33 percent thought it important to keep up with political affiars. Considering these views, the college experience cannot be called a failure if all graduates do not find related jobs.

SOCIAL BENEFITS

Most people agree that postsecondary education serves a number of functions from which society as a whole benefits. Unfortunately, these functions have been more frequently verbalized than quantified. Some have argued that a more educated society is one in which democracy is more likely to flourish. Violent crime is lower in an educated society. Gross national product (GNP) is generally higher in societies where a greater proportion of the citizens have large amounts of education. Although poverty is certain to exist regardless of the level of GNP, it is difficult to argue that national income or welfare could be improved by educating fewer people.

Even in earlier periods, when a much smaller proportion of the nation's youth attended college, many graduates took jobs that did not specifically require their college training. Most of the scientific manpower for the space effort was not new graduates, but rather people who worked elsewhere when labor demands in science were low. The move toward equal access to college education has increased the opportunity for more citizens to participate in the "lottery" for the relatively few related jobs. But whatever the criterion for hiring, those with more education, compared with others of the same age and other similarities, have broadened their perspectives, expanded their capacity for involvement in the political process, and increased their appreciation of the arts and a multitude of leisure-time activities.

In considering the impact of college, society must acknowledge the problem of accomplishing work that requires vocational training, or manual skills rather than the intellectual skills developed in college. Rather than arguing, as some do, that certain groups should be sent to vocational school and others to college, or that this decision perpetuates a class system, the full postsecondary sector should provide a variety of skills, vocational and intellectual, to all participants. This might enable the plumber to enjoy opera and the philosopher to fix his drainpipe.

To get its dirty work done, society must redefine manual tasks—nonintellectual tasks—as necessary and valuable. It might try to assure that most individuals perform some of these nonintellectual tasks for a few years, perhaps during youth or some later period in life. A social model somewhat like the military draft might be useful. It could be modified so an explicit learning experience would be integrated with the tasks for which people were drafted.

Those in nonintellectual jobs could have opportunities, if they desired, to expand the intellectual aspects of their nonworking life. Some critics might be surprised to find that a large number of people in manual, "nonthinking" jobs are satisfied with their lives, even if they think they might be happier in a different job. Manual workers do not generally bring their problems home. A clearly separable work and leisure life, with ample gratification during the nonworking periods, might attract certain individuals to jobs that are now "undesirable." With adequate notice that certain courses are for nonvocational reinforcement and with adequate salary for manual jobs (as in the craft unions), many people could both benefit from college and hold nonintellectual jobs.

IDENTIFICATION OF A GOOD JOB

Clearly, there are more purposes of higher education than merely providing students with specific job-related skills. Nevertheless, one purpose of college is to enable graduates to get a "good job." A basic problem in the recent criticism of higher education is that there is no general agreement on what a good job is—or on what a "bad" job is. Many observations on good jobs come from intellectuals who judge a job by what they might like to do. This study revealed that what is a good job to some people is not a good job to others. For example, only 8 percent of those in middle-level administration who graduated from arts and humanities fields are satisfied with their jobs. However, 64 percent of those with bachelor's degrees in the social sciences are satisfied, and 87 percent of those with bachelor's in history are satisfied with middle-level administration. Similarly, only 11 percent of those with a bachelor's in English who are communications specialists are satisfied with their job, but 70 percent of those with a degree in the social sciences are satisfied. Specific jobs held by people with different majors may differ substantially, even though they fall under the same generic occupational heading. But, apparently, certain types of occupations are satisfying to particular individuals and not to others. There is no such thing as a good job that is good for everyone.

Certain characteristics, however, are associated with job satisfaction. Some are outcomes, such as salary and status; others are features of the job itself, such as good working conditions or relationships with the supervisor.

External Characteristics

One aspect of a job clearly associated with satisfaction is salary level. That high-paying jobs are better jobs has been traditionally accepted. Critics are challenging this view today, maintaining that employers have a responsibility to provide intellectual or social stimulation on the job. Most nonmonetary amenities provided to workers cost money. Hence, there will probably be trade-offs between salary and other costly job attributes. Jobs that provide opportunities for additional training within or outside the company, jobs that provide social clubs or company libraries, for example, probably pay less than jobs where such amenities are not available. If employees were given a choice between higher salaries or more esoteric fringe benefits, they probably would opt for the salaries.

In interpreting data on the value of education, the first question is, What is a large number and what is a small number? For example, the survey of college graduates revealed that 45 percent think they use the content of their undergraduate major in work almost always or frequently. This figure can lead sympathetic commentators to argue that colleges and universities are doing very well if almost half those with bachelor's degrees find jobs in which they use the substance of their major. But critics can argue that over half those with degrees are not in jobs that use their training. Similarly, the survey of 1974 freshmen indicated that roughly 55 percent think they will find a job in their preferred field upon graduation. Does this mean that a large number of students are going to college even though they do not think they will find a job they will like upon graduation? Or does it imply that a majority of freshmen enter college anticipating that they will find a job they want? This same survey indicated that 55 percent of the men and 36 percent of the women think it very important that they be financially well off in the future. Of course, this means that 45 percent of the men and 64 percent of the women do not think it is very important. Is it more correct to argue that today's college freshmen seek financial security, or that a large number do not think financial security is very important? Most "hard" data are subject to at least two interpretations.

A good job should enable people to achieve their goals. Of course, this begs the question of what the goals are. Many goals stated by students when they begin college are probably not going to be achieved easily in any job. For example, the two objectives most frequently considered essential or very important by most men and women freshmen in 1974 were to be an authority in their field and to develop a philosophy of life. Jobs in which people achieve these goals are difficult to find. Those who become authorities will probably do so irrespective of their jobs, and developing a philosophy of life is probably beside the point for most jobs.

It is also hard to get realistic admissions of a person's goals. For example, youth may be unwilling to admit the "crass" objective of making money. Some evidence has indicated that when jobseekers have the option of jobs with current or future high-income prospects, these jobs are selected over those with other attributes. Even if jobs should be tailored to help individuals achieve personal goals, this adjustment will be virtually impossible unless true goals can be determined. Moreover, goals change as individuals mature, gain experience, and accumulate responsibilities.

Some think that good jobs are those that are socially meaningful, a useless definition. Who defines what is socially meaningful? Is a job socially meaningful if productivity is high but national income equality is hindered by highly productive individuals making exceptionally high salaries? Is a job socially meaningful if one can espouse liberal causes therein? There is virtually no way to achieve consensus on the definition of a socially meaningful job.

A more concrete aspect of a good job is the ability to maximize productivity in terms of output, profit to the firm, or other aims of the employer. This definition enables objective measurement of productivity and output on the one hand and identifies the business firm as the entity that will specify the aspects of productivity on the other. However, certain individuals might maximize their productivity both to business firms and to the larger society by undertaking jobs with minimum amounts of other characteristics, such as being socially meaningful. Also, how is an individual to be placed in a "good job"—defined as one that maximizes his productivity—if his comparative advantage is a manual skill and if manual jobs, as a matter of course, are "bad jobs"?

Many people think that jobs with high status are good jobs. Once again, the question is, who is defining a high-status job? If intellectuals continue to maintain that jobs requiring manual or vocational skills are low status, it will be impossible to structure a labor market in which satisfied employees work in vocational and manual areas. Rather than viewing job status from outside, a company might be able to develop internal job status for those in lower positions. Labor unions have developed administrative hierarchies that include foremen and other administrators so individuals on the assembly line have internal job status even though their specific jobs are not viewed by the outside world as high status. Perhaps if internal responsibilities for low-level policy-making or decisions on procedures or operations could be given to workers in traditionally low-status jobs to increase their own job's development and the corporate policy, they might view their jobs as "good" even though outsiders would not classify the jobs as high status.

A job may also be viewed as "good" in relation to other jobs an individual has held, or to jobs held by an individual's peers or family, or to what the individual "expected." The status of a job may also depend on who held it previously.

Internal Characteristics

Other components of a good job are internal characteristics that can be brought into almost any work situation. To the extent that jobs possess these characteristics, workers view their jobs as relatively good, without regard to salary, external status, and social meaning.

Jobs with congenial work relationships, variety rather than repetition, and flexible hours, which allow individuals to define their own tasks within reason, may be relatively "good" jobs. Traditionally, these characteristics have been associated with jobs with high salary and status, social meaning, and overall satisfaction. However, there is no reason why more jobs could not be restructured to include these characteristics and thereby become attractive to more college graduates. With the addition of congenial relationships, variety, and flexibility, more educated workers might feel satisfied, despite the absence of some other job characteristics they ostensibly desire. The question is, do college graduates prefer jobs with high salary, status, meaning, and satisfaction because these jobs have congeniality, variety, flexibility, and independence; or do jobs with the latter characteristics generally lead to high salary, status, and so on?

Jobs with upward mobility are considered good jobs. Traditionally, business enterprises have allowed people in certain jobs to move up the status ladder, whereas other jobs have been dead end. This inequity is a significant complaint of critics of the structure of the world of work, since certain "bad" tasks must be performed and the labor force is obtaining more education. The dead-end job phenomenon could be solved: If promotion were made after considering all employees, not just line employees, dead-end jobs could, in a sense, be defined away. Upward mobility should not mean that anyone, regardless of skills and aptitudes, has a right to obtain a higher job, but rather that no one is in a position where his skills go unrecognized. Few positions, including stoker of the steel furnace, exist where some superiors do not view the habits and skills of workers under them. Indeed, many companies have two types of office boys: Those with a bachelor's degree are called junior trainees; those with less than a college education are called messengers. If these artificial titles were removed, both jobs could be filled by people of ability and potential, and people in both jobs could be promoted. Internal dead-end jobs are not a problem of the educational system, but of the formalism and traditionalism of the work structure. If business finds too few individuals for "bad" jobs and education finds too few jobs for graduates, the two could solve the problem: Business could redefine jobs and review individuals for promotion regardless of title, while educators could encourage people to begin their careers in low-status jobs with the assurance that promotion is possible.

External upward mobility is somewhat more difficult to achieve, since it requires the acceptance by one employer of job descriptions and evaluations by other employers. A research scientist in one firm is clearly more visible than a junior-clerk trainee to those making hiring decisions in other firms. However, once it is recognized internally that people in low-status jobs are qualified for higher positions, the most qualified in those jobs probably will be sought by other firms.

Education/Job Relationship

An important criterion of a good job is full utilization of skills, sometimes called full employment, or matching people to jobs. Traditionally, where skills are fully utilized and workers are matched to appropriate jobs, the jobs are good for the workers and the workers are good for the jobs.

Chapter 3 discussed in detail the meaning of a "related" job: There are many dimensions of relationship, and these differ according to major and occupation.

In attempting to explain individual differences in both income and job satisfaction, after accounting for such individual characteristics as grade-point average, type of institution attended, years on the job, and the like, whether or not an individual thinks he is working in the field for which he was trained adds virtually nothing to the ability of the model to explain these differences. The whole premise of the education-work partnership is based on the belief that those using their training are more satisfied and earn more. However, it appears from this study that whether or not one uses one's education on the job does not significantly affect one's job satisfaction or income, after holding constant other characteristics of the individual.

Good jobs may be those that allow intellectual development and thinking. Clearly, a plumber or an electrician must think on the job. Indeed, some of the most creative thinking is by electricians trying to figure out how to rewire a house. If the process of thinking became respectable, rather than respect accruing to those who think about certain things, many necessary jobs could be redefined as good jobs. One manifestation of job snobbery has been an increasing shortage of people to fill manual and vocational jobs. Disproportionately high wages are tending to counterbalance the nonintellectuality of certain jobs.

A final solution to the problem of bright people in less intellectual jobs might be in the relationship between work and leisure. There is nothing to preclude a person with an eight-hour-a-day routine job from spending nonworking hours in intellectual pursuits. Hence, an effective definition of a good job might be a job where you do not have to work much to earn an adequate living so you have ample time and resources to enjoy your leisure.

The age and generation of a worker is also a consideration in evaluating job quality. Certain jobs by their very nature are held by older people who have had the experience to qualify for them. For example, if being one's own boss is an important characteristic of a good job, few recent graduates would feel they had a good job. Although many new entrants to the labor force can work in a bank, for example, a new employee is unlikely to be president. Also, critics should not compare younger and older employees in banking or any other occupation to see if one is more satisfied and then argue that today's youth are more demanding because the older generation has satisfying jobs and youth do not. Clearly, the proper comparison is between the youth or older worker of today and their respective age groups of earlier generations.

Some maintain that even when today's youth are compared with earlier generations, current youth are more dissatisfied. However, a recent study that evaluated job satisfaction from 1958 to 1973 indicated that, for the past 15 years, younger workers have been less satisfied in their jobs than older workers. Thus, the alleged decline in job satisfaction of younger workers has not been empirically substantiated. Some predict that as youth become the older workers, they will be more dissatisfied than today's older workers. Those who entered the labor force in the 1950s remember well the problems their parents had during the depression and base their values and aspirations on these observations. A job with income security, longevity, and perhaps upward mobility was the first order of importance to this generation. New entrants in the 1960s did not know about earlier depressions, since most came from relatively affluent backgrounds. They assumed a certain minimum level of earning power and job security and felt free to assert that other aspects of jobs were of primary importance. The aims and perspectives of youth are probably influenced by the economic and social setting when they begin their careers. Some evidence indicated that college students and new entrants are reverting to the more basic job requirements and becoming concerned about job security and income. It is unsound to extrapolate into the future a trend between the

1950s and 1960s which shows an increasing concern by new entrants for the noneconomic aspects of work. That almost 50 percent of the 1974 college freshmen think financial well-being is an important goal implies a continuation of traditional job values rather than a movement toward enrichment.

EDUCATION AS A JOB CREDENTIAL

Regardless of how many good jobs are available, as long as the number of individuals is greater than the number of jobs, some allocative decision will be required. Those who make hiring decisions must select people to fill certain jobs, and in so doing preclude others.

Given a number of applicants for a particular job, there are alternatives for deciding whom to hire. Recent critiques of the job market have asked: How does society determine who gets the good jobs? The implication is that some decision-making network in society establishes norms for hiring. Except for the military draft, now ended, there has been little mandating of people into specific jobs. Workers are neither allocated to nor awarded jobs in some random fashion such as a lottery. The hiring process involves decisions by potential employees to apply for jobs and decisions by employers about whom to hire.

Employees make an earlier decision to acquire training that will probably be useful in specific jobs. This study asked workers whether they decided upon their career before college, during college, at graduation, or after. Apparently, people select their careers over a relatively wide time period. Those who choose their field before college prepare for that specific career. Some attend college to obtain general aptitudes and skills useful in many jobs. Others acquire competencies during college and then decide that those competencies will lead to a desirable career.

Time is a strong factor in the probability of using education in a career. The earlier a particular career is selected, the greater the likelihood of feeling that one is using his education in his job. After preparing for particular jobs through specific or general college training, people apply for positions they think are "relatively good."

Narrowed Criteria

When there is more than one applicant for a job, an employer must "discriminate." Although "discriminate" has a negative social connotation, *Webster's New Collegiate Dictionary* defines it as "making a distinction" or differentiating. Employers attempt to differentiate among potential employees by criteria relevant to success in the job. Recently, employers have based decisions on such differentiating traits as sex, race, age, and education. Slowly, these are being legislated out as hiring criteria.

If age, sex, and race are illegal criteria, one may assume they are irrelevant to value on a job. Critics have attacked the practice of basing hiring decisions on individual educational credentials. Traditionally, those with more education have been considered more productive, so an educational criterion for hiring was logical. The validity of an educational credential depends on whether educated people are, indeed, more productive.

Some have argued that if one's work is not related to one's education, education as a hiring credential is irrelevant: If an employer required a mathematics degree for a job typing poetry, that requirement would be hard to justify. But if an employer required a college education for a secretarial position, the validity of that requirement would be clearer. One would assume that an individual with a bachelor's would be more skilled with grammar and English composition, which would assure higher quality work than that of a person with less competence in the language.

The question remains whether an educational credential implies use of specific knowledge obtained in college or whether it reflects general skills that must be demonstrated to obtain a bachelor's degree and which would be useful in the job.

Research on worker productivity has shown that educational attainment is a significant factor. Unfortunately, the measure of productivity has usually been earnings. It is unclear whether those with more education are paid more because they are more productive, or because employers discriminate unjustifiably in favor of those with more education. Most economists who believe that the system of competitive capitalism works have concluded that employers pay more to educated people because they really are more productive.

It is not important that workers with more education are more productive because they use the specific content of their college courses on the job. The more educated workers possess many traits that are useful, even when their specific studies are not. Those who obtain a college degree may be more motivated, persistent, ambitious, and hard-working. They may be better able to achieve objectives, since they possess more traits that enhance on-the-job productivity.

Refined Differentiation

Rather than eliminating educational level as a screen, more detailed educational credentials should be developed. Employers could consider not only the level of degree but also the quality of an applicant's institution and major field. If one could show that individuals from certain institutions are more productive because certain characteristics are required for graduation, or that individuals in certain majors possess certain characteristics, one could refine educational credentials. If education is a proxy for productive characteristics, employers could use tests to determine whether applicants possess characteristics that enhance productivity. The cost of testing, however, might be quite high.

Employers should never rely totally on educational attainment as a hiring criterion but use it with other screening devices, such as personal interviews. If education were totally ignored, however, the same individuals would probably get the jobs, because they would possess more productive traits associated with achievement in higher education. This is particularly true as access to colleges (to "good" colleges particularly) expands.

In the relationship of people to jobs, the problem is not that the wrong people are getting the good jobs, but that there are too few jobs that certain people view as good, considering the many people thought to deserve good jobs. As long as applicants outnumber jobs, some differentiating mechanism must be employed. Educational achievement is one satisfactory credential.

8

SUMMARY AND
RECOMMENDATIONS

This study was based on data from a 1974 follow-up survey of a 1961 college freshman cohort. Most respondents had been in the labor force for eight or nine years. About half indicated they are working in jobs closely related to their major; another 25 percent think they are in jobs somewhat related, while 25 percent think they hold jobs not at all related to their college major. Of those in unrelated jobs, about 90 percent indicated that they hold these jobs voluntarily. That is, the large majority of those not using their college training directly has not been pushed out of related jobs but, rather, has been pulled into more desirable situations.

Almost 60 percent of the respondents are very satisfied with their jobs. Those in jobs closely related to their major are slightly more satisfied than those in unrelated jobs, but the difference is small. Only 5 percent of respondents are not at all satisfied with their present job and these are mainly individuals involuntarily holding jobs unrelated to their major. In an attempt to explain individual differences in both job satisfaction and income, adding various dimensions of relationship of job to major contributed almost nothing to the explanation of individual differences.

The content of major courses is never used in the job by 10 percent, while 48 percent use the content frequently or almost always. However, college education serves purposes other than providing knowledge from courses to be used on the job. It is a credential for securing the first or current job, although it is less influential for promotions. Workers think their college education identifies them as potentially valuable workers even when the work is unrelated. In addition, college provides general skills not specifically related to their jobs. The development of intellect and general knowledge and the ability to define life goals are among the nonspecific end results of the college experience. In addition, college provides non-work-related values, such as enjoyment of the college experience at the time, political awareness, and development of specific values and tastes.

Of the respondents, 73 percent said college is very useful in increasing general knowledge, while 43 percent said it provides the ability to think clearly. College provides knowledge and skills useful on the current job for 38 percent. It provides leadership ability for 22 percent and contacts that helped get the current job for 5 percent. Sixty-nine percent think college increases the chances of finding a good job.

In addition to using the content of major and nonmajor courses, the respondents had other perceptions of the relationship of job to major. Those who found that college trained them to do a lot of things they are not doing on the job are less likely to think they are in a related job, even if they are using the content of their courses. Those who supervise or work with people trained in their field are more likely to think they are in a related job. Those who think that college gave them skills and knowledge useful on their job, even if these were not provided in courses, are more likely to think they are in a related job. Apparently, the usefulness of college in later work depends not only on course content but also on other college experiences, such as dormitory living, fraternity life, social life, and extracurricular activities and the particular design of the job.

Only 32 percent of the respondents think their skills are fully utilized on the job. This fact does not indicate a failure of college training. Indeed, this feeling is pervasive among those in the most directly related jobs. Even people in high-level or prestigious jobs think they have many skills that are not used. These talents were not necessarily acquired in college.

Individual differences in perceptions of a related job and the extent to which relationship of job to major contributes to job satisfaction and income vary substantially by individual major and by type of occupation. The percentage of respondents which uses the major frequently or almost always, by major, includes education 61 percent, business 55 percent, engineering 49 percent, English 44 percent, economics 37 percent, and other social sciences 24 percent. There are also substantial differences in perceptions by sex. More women than men are in low-level jobs. However, women's criteria for evaluating a job as satisfactory seem to be less stringent than those of men.

Some 45 percent of the respondents recommend business administration for training for a job like theirs. The second most useful field, recommended by 32 percent, is English. This selection probably means the need to read, write, and communicate rather than a deep knowledge of Shakespeare. Psychology is recommended by 31 percent, which probably reflects the need to get along with people, while 28 percent recommend economics, which probably reflects the need for business-related skills.

Some 56 percent of the men and 37 percent of the women think their job fits their long-range goals. This finding contrasts with some recent comment that dissatisfaction with the world of work is pervasive among recent college graduates.

Apparently, there are no clear criteria to define a good job. All jobs are not good jobs for everyone, but to someone, a particular job will be satisfactory. Perceptions depend on life and career goals, which vary from person to person. Goals are hard to measure, and some are not recognized or revealed by a large number of respondents.

Some jobs need less than college-level skills. However, if a worker has more than the minimum required skills, his job may be modified to take advantage of additional talents. Some jobs require skills and knowledge that build on the college experience but are not taught in college. Many individuals select their careers after college. Certain jobs require skills that must be learned on the job. Of course, some jobs must be selected early since they require college courses. But, almost everyone picks up additional skills on the job or in formal programs. Almost no one says that no additional training beyond college is required for work. Certain jobs do not require specific college training and can be held by those unable to find related jobs or unable to decide on a college program to prepare them for work. But, in any case, the college experience may be useful.

RELEVANCE OF THE SAMPLE TO THE PRESENT "CRISIS"

All things considered, the majority of those who were college freshmen in 1961 and who obtained only a B.A. degree are well satisfied with their current jobs. A significant number are using their college training at work, even after eight or nine years; those who are not using their training, for the most part, are doing so voluntarily. These results fly in the face of recent discussion that a great majority of college graduates are dissatisfied with their jobs and are not using their college education. The sample in this study comprised individuals in the labor force for a number of years. Most new entrants to the labor market take jobs that are not typical of those they will hold after several years. An analysis of new entrants to the labor force might have results unfairly biased toward dissatisfaction and nonutilization of college training. The same individuals who are dissatisfied now because they are not using their training will probably get more satisfying jobs and make more use of their college training in a couple of years. A literature review uncovered evidence that new entrants have always been more dissatisfied than those with several years of experience. Most new entrants have always been more dissatisfied than those with several years of experience. Most new entrants want to be bank presidents but start out as clerks. Hence, the proper evaluation of the usefulness of college for jobs comes from studying people who have been in the labor force for some years, rather than from focusing on new entrants.

In addition, recent discussions have concerned college graduates who entered the labor force during a severe recession. It is unrealistic to extrapolate from the most recent years to the future when the business sector will pick up and more and better jobs will be available. Also, a much larger proportion of the population currently holds bachelor's degrees than has ever before been the case. As more individuals enter the labor force armed with a B.A., it is inevitable that they will be forced into jobs that were not traditionally jobs for college graduates. It remains to be seen whether individual aspirations and talents will be dampened or whether the expectations and requirements of certain jobs will be expanded.

In the depression of the 1930s, workers with many years of experience were made painfully aware of the economic crisis by pay declines, layoffs, and inability to find new jobs. Today, these effects are only observed at the margin, that is, new entrants are the ones hurt, whereas experienced workers seem satisfied in appropriate jobs.

MEANING OF UNDEREMPLOYMENT

Although few college graduates fail to find jobs, fear is growing that this group is being forced into more jobs characterized as underemployment. Inadequate thought has been given to the meaning and measurement of the concept of underemployment. To determine whether college education is a wise investment, it is necessary to evaluate the degree of underemployment among college graduates.

The most literal definition of underemployment includes the concept that the individual is not working at the type of job for which he is trained. This study has questioned whether even the most specific college major trains individuals for particular jobs or whether college provides a way of thinking, communicating, and learning which makes the graduate an appropriate employee in a wide variety of settings. A broader but related concept is the full utilization of a graduate's skills and talents. Although utilization of specific course content in jobs does seem substantial for many, individuals indicated that they do not think all their skills and talents are being utilized. Most perceive full utilization of skills as use of a variety of talents, both innate and learned, that go well beyond the specifics acquired in college courses.

To deprecate college training because of underemployment as defined above is difficult. For example, look at the person with a B.A. in classics who is a bank president. In a sense he is not using his college training and probably thinks many of his skills are not utilized in his work. However, who would say that a bank president, making perhaps $250,000 a year, is underemployed? Is this individual a victim of society? Has he been misled by the promises that college would provide him with a job without underemployment?

This example suggests some other definitions of underemployment: Perhaps those who are not satisfied with their work are underemployed. Research on the psychology of satisfaction with work and with other aspects of life is inadequate. Perhaps individuals who are dissatisfied with their jobs feel this way because they are generally dissatisfied with their lives. Those in the most menial and unpleasant jobs could feel satisfied, if the whole sum of their lives was fulfilling and they were generally happy. Job satisfaction cannot be looked at in a vacuum.

Another aspect of underemployment might be relative income. In this country, the perception is that college graduates should earn more than those without degrees. But how much more? There is a vast literature on the determinants of income. If there are great shortages of certain skilled labor, such as plumbers and electricians, quite possibly these craftsmen will be able to raise their rates and earn much more than those with a college education. All those earning a relatively high income should not be defined as fully employed; neither are all those earning relatively low incomes underemployed.

Finally, observers have indicated that a worker is underemployed if he holds a job requiring lower minimum skills than those he possesses. Once again one must ask about particular jobs and individuals rather than generic categories of jobs with general definitions of skill requirements. Although a secretarial job might be defined as requiring only two years of high school, it is quite apparent that secretaries with more education are performing tasks that could not be performed by those with a minimum education, although the two individuals are holding jobs with the same title.

RECONSIDERATION OF THE VALUES OF COLLEGE

This study weakens arguments that college is no longer valuable as preparation for work: A great deal of college training is viewed by workers as useful in their jobs. College also serves a credentialing function, since workers with more education are more desirable for almost every job regardless of requirements. As more of the population gets college-level training, the negative credential value of not having a college education becomes dominant.

Since this study focused on people in the labor force for a number of years, it does not fully contradict arguments about the reduced value of college for recent graduates. Given this, institutions of higher education and those who support them should begin rethinking the worth of college. During the time when the mere possession of a college degree assured graduates of a good job, the universities became complacent and based arguments for expanded funding and growth on the work-related values of college. The research literature reflects this trend: Much more effort has been put into empirically substantiating job-related benefits than into efforts to document empirically that college provides a wide range of other benefits as well. The question now becomes: What will the colleges sell to legislators and others who have supported higher education in the past but are now skeptical about the work-related benefits of college training?

A reconsideration of the values of college and the various ways a college education may be beneficial to individuals and the broader society is necessary. In the first place, the course content-job requirement interface should not be the only focus in evaluating the work-related benefits of college. College can contribute in various ways to job performance. The development of values and attitudes by graduates is probably of more use to employers than specific knowledge. Experiences that develop values and attitudes might result from extracurricular activities, dormitory living, fraternity life, or merely the discipline of getting up early to pass an attendance check at an eight o'clock class.

Second, college may help a graduate get a good job even if the job is not directly related to the college major. A college education does serve as a screening device. Today, that screen may have been raised from the mere possession of a degree to achievement in college, a particular major, or institutional quality. If those who attend college are more qualified than those who do not and employers use evidence of college attendance in hiring decisions, perhaps the colleges should explicitly recognize this fact. Colleges could be of use to employers and society by evaluating students in terms of criteria useful in work. An evaluation would enable the colleges to control the decision-making process of employers better by preventing them from deciding which aspects of college should be used as a screen. Students' attainment in the noncourse aspects of the college experience, as well as in the curriculum (measured with grade-point average), might be certified.

In addition to recognizing that college can contribute to job performance in a variety of ways and that the credentialing function is not counterproductive, supporters of higher education must further explore the impacts of college which go beyond the job market. Not all college effects are job related. Students attend college for various reasons, having nothing to do with work. Table 8.1 shows important life goals of 1961 freshmen when they were surveyed in 1971 (El-Khawas and Bisconti 1974). The data are weighted to represent the total freshman class of 1961. These responses probably reflect attitudes in 1971 rather than actual intentions of individuals when they entered college. By 1971, most respondents were much more aware of the world of work than they were when they entered college. Despite this bias, the respondents did not place work-related goals at the top of their list of priorities. The most popular goal is to raise a family, one generally irrelevant to job traits. Second is the opportunity for hobbies and leisure activities, also irrelevant to job characteristics (except that certain jobs do not require after-hours work). However, third is the opportunity to help others in difficulty, which might imply that certain

TABLE 8.1

Life Goals of 1961 Cohort, by Sex (in percentages)

Essential or Very Important Goals	Total (N = 693,512)	Men (N = 397,902)	Women (N = 295,610)
Become accomplished in a performing art	14	11	17
Become an authority in my field	48	57	35
Obtain recognition from colleagues	40	50	27
Be very well off financially	38	47	27
Help others in difficulty	59	54	66
Become a community leader	16	19	11
Make a theoretical contribution to science	6	8	3
Write original works (poems, and so forth)	7	6	8
Be successful in own business	27	37	13
Raise a family	78	76	81
Become involved in programs to clean up the environment	36	35	37
Develop ways to use science and technology in improving the quality of life	33	38	28
Be involved in efforts to improve health, reduce illness	37	34	41
Engage in hobbies and leisure activities	64	62	67

types of jobs, such as those in social service and health, would be most satisfying. Being well-off financially ranks in the middle of the list. Although goals involving intellectual or artistic creativity are somewhat important, most important objectives are either altruistic or completely unrelated to work. The question then arises: Is it necessary to stress work-related benefits of college when the consumers of college services do not state that their most important goals are work related?

A literature is developing on characteristics of the educational experience which enable students subsequently to earn higher incomes and obtain better jobs. Many of these job-related characteristics also have implications for other aspects of life. Certainly, the increased knowledge gained in school is productive. However, increased socialization and willingness to take risks and to innovate are other income-incrementing characteristics that might be obtained from the educational experience and also affect other aspects of life.

More and more, nonpecuniary rewards from extra schooling are also being recognized. Some argue that those with more education are more efficient consumers and that they use their time more effectively. Others claim that enjoyment from reading a good novel is greater for those with more education.

Benefits from higher education also accrue to society as a whole. Universities should not ignore these advantages in making the case for continued support for higher learning. Some of these benefits are shared by the student and society in general, while others accrue more to society than to the individual. Traditionally, for example, the more educated society is, allegedly, a better functioning democracy. This might benefit the better-educated individual only slightly. However, education of those who later become parents benefits subsequent generations of children. There is evidence that children of more educated mothers, for example, ultimately become more successful than children of less educated mothers, controlling for a large number of other factors. In a sense this is a social return.

Certain benefits of college which accrue either to the individual or to the broader society might be evident during college, at graduation, or perhaps not until many years later. There is consumption value in attending particularly enjoyable classes. Students' attitudes might change between the time they enter and leave college. However, the recognizable value of learning how to learn and the development of a philosophy of life might come many years after graduation.

In sum, the case for higher education must be taken up by the institutions of higher education and their supporters. This case must be made with arguments broader than just the interface between education and jobs.

PROVIDING INFORMATION TO STUDENTS

Colleges and universities continue to be ineffective in selling themselves as national assets yielding benefits well beyond those job related in the narrowest sense. Part of this failure is due to the universities' inadequate provision of a wide range of information to students. Part of the universities' public relations problems today result because, when information is not provided, critics infer that the universities are less successful than they really are. That is, when universities do not talk about the total benefits that result from attendance, some interpret this to mean that even those within institutions of higher education do not believe that such benefits exist.

State and federal governments have recently begun forcing universities to be accountable, that is, to show what happens to students upon graduation.

However, this requirement has been turned directly into attempts to show how many students are placed in jobs and where. The universities must take the lead in providing additional information on other outcomes of education. This will not only encourage students to continue enrolling despite publicity about bad job prospects, but also weaken arguments about the declining value of college generally.

The universities could also provide students with much other information currently absent. First, students should know how to train in college for jobs. They should receive more guidance on an appropriate curriculum. They should be told which aspects of college are useful in jobs. Students should also know that, despite their college education, most jobs will require additional preparation. Many skills are learned on the job. Students should know that flexible training and the acquisition of flexible skills and broadly applicable experience are desirable during the college years. The time is past when one can rely on professors of English or physics who preach that the only road to truth, employment, and happiness is to study the specific courses they teach.

Students should be encouraged to continue college despite publicity about a declining labor market for graduates. When everybody has a degree, the risks of not having one are great. At the same time, students must know about the probabilistic nature of the job market: A B.A. in chemistry does not assure the graduate of a high-powered research job, and a B.A. in classics may not guarantee any job at all. If students know about job prospects and the inherent risks and still choose to enroll in college, then they make that decision freely and honestly. The college is at fault only when it lures students by assurances of jobs to provide employment for obsolete faculty. If students are attracted to college because non-work-related benefits are stressed, their enrollment is rational and should be encouraged.

Students must be kept informed about the labor market and where the shortages and surpluses are. They must be knowledgeable about the employment rates of previous and current graduates of the institution, realizing that times might be quite different when they graduate four or more years in the future. Information about labor markets must be based on empirical evidence, not on anecdotes or personal biases. Advocates of the continued growth of higher education must be challenged to provide an empirical base for allegations of non-work-related benefits as well.

Institutions should consider how this information is conveyed to students. Currently, it is available in somewhat random fashion from counselors, faculty, administrators, media, and a few government agencies or private research groups. It is almost impossible for the naive high school graduate or college freshman to distill information available in so many ways at varying times and with such a wide degree of certainty. Some institutions are considering restructuring student services to provide a consistent and continuous flow of information.

CHANGES REQUIRED IN INSTITUTIONS

Most colleges and universities have separate offices for career placement, counseling, cooperative education, veterans' counseling, part-time work and work-study, and freshman orientation. This separation is ruinous: It leads to fragmented information which, at times, is inconsistent, misdirected, or untimely. The flow of information from the time of application to exit should be coordinated within an institution and treated as a single process.

This study implies that a common core curriculum at the college level should be reinstituted. Rather than the traditional three R's of the elementary schools, or the traditional college core of humanities, arts, and sciences, the new core might be composed of business, psychology, and English courses. These common areas might better prepare all students to face an increasingly technical and business-oriented world. Courses in each field could give them some of the humanistic insights that were once the trademark of a college graduate.

But curricular revision without modification of course content would be futile. For engineers who need French for international business, the course cannot be eighteenth-century French literature. Courses in basic principles of business, psychology, and written communications would be appropriate, with optional courses in more applied areas of the core or in more abstract aspects of the same subjects. With at least two courses in each of these fields, the curriculum would enable humanists to gain some entry-level job skills and engineers to develop a broader perspective than the technical competencies they now get.

The question immediately arises: Are departmental curriculum committees able to design courses to serve the intentions of the reconstituted core curriculum? Some colleges have adopted the principle that freshman and sophomore courses should not be controlled by departments. Some institutions have instituted an undergraduate dean for the freshman and sophomore years. This puts an individual in control of curriculum who can see the offerings from the viewpoint of institutional objectives.

Certainly institutions should consider utilizing existing courses and faculty to provide these revised courses and desired skills. As enrollments decline, both because of demographics and economics, some faculty will have trouble filling classes. The truly successful colleges might be those that attract students into classes on Shakespeare because these classes not only discuss how to read Shakespeare but also analyze how Shakespeare wrote; and into mathematics classes, not only to learn quadratic forms but also because some examples involve basic accounting. Many faculty will resist this need to revise courses to make them relevant to the real world. However, if they have no choice, this goal might be achieved. That is, students will be encouraged to acquire training in general work skills (English, writing, mathematics, accounting), regardless of whether they major in French literature or engineering. Basic skills lead to better job prospects regardless of the supply-demand situation for particular jobs and majors. The alternative of preserving the current freshman and sophomore curriculum could lead to plummeting enrollments in certain fields, and the opportunity to teach the traditional courses would vanish.

DECLINING ROLE OF FACULTY LEADERSHIP

The suggested curricular changes may appear simple to effect. The need for more job-related course content seems obvious to those who recognize that the graduates in the deepest trouble are those in the most esoteric fields. However, one must recognize that faculty interest may conflict directly with the interests of students and the broader society.

In the first place, faculty are understandably reluctant to revise course content and change lectures after presenting materials in a certain way for a number of years. A change would involve an effort that is generally not rewarded in institutions where publication is the overwhelming criterion for promotion and salary increments, to say nothing of status with colleagues. Many faculty believe that what they have been doing is valuable. Courses, as they are usually designed, are rich with tradition, have been tested over a long period, and have turned out graduates who have generally succeeded in work and life. Some course revision requires different knowledge and talents than those possessed by faculty currently teaching basic English, foreign languages, economics, or psychology. Much retooling would be necessary in certain cases.

The second problem arises if faculty are expected to advise students to broaden their choices so their curriculum includes more courses useful in the world of work. The danger for a professor of classical literature if he recommends that his students sample psychology or business is that the students might decide that psychology or business is either more interesting or more marketable than classics. The classics professor could lose a student rather than gain a student who knows classics but has broader skills.

Most institutions are under pressure to keep enrollments up. If enrollments in a particular field decline, new faculty hiring becomes impossible and layoffs may result. Not only does this prevent the introduction of new blood and new colleagues into a department, but many times it also threatens the jobs of existing nontenured faculty and in certain cases tenured faculty. In this case, what is good for the student and perhaps even the institution as a whole conflicts with what is good for a particular department. If the core curriculum became widely acceptable, overall institutional enrollments might rise or at least not fall as much. However, this increase might be at the expense of certain departments that were not providing marketable skills or experiences deemed valuable by students and potential employers.

Course and curricular revision, then, cannot be met by the self-generating action of the faculty. This point is important because, during the prosperous 1960s, faculty were given a great deal of control over curriculum in the universities. It is now time for top-level administrators to recognize the problems and the solutions and to take charge anew of the decision-making mechanisms to implement these changes. These changes will require strong leaders who are willing to challenge the faculty if that need arises.

Although certain changes probably will have to be mandated from above, college leaders might consider how institutional reward structures could be modified to produce incentives for faculty, staff, and other administrators to accept the changes. The most obvious incentive is rewarding faculty with promotion and salary increases for curricular revision and innovative methods of teaching relevant skills. Certainly the development of an English literature course that results in improved writing skills could be considered as valuable as an article published in an academic journal.

The success a department has in placing students in jobs or in obtaining indications of satisfaction with the curriculum might be the criteria upon which budgets are determined. One of the most devastating occurrences in higher education has been the enrollment-driven budgetary allocation system. If a department chairman could see that it is more important that his students obtain a well-rounded education by taking courses outside their main field than it is merely to maintain his class enrollments, he might be willing to settle for lower enrollments and more broadly educated graduates.

Strong top-level leadership is essential in these times. Administrators must be aware of the problems faced by graduates attempting to enter the labor market without marketable skills and the problems that result for the universities. They must also be convinced that there are solutions to these problems. Changed incentives within the institutions would be a big step toward solving the problems.

Those who argue that college is no longer worth the price might be overstating their case. However, this is not to suggest that there is no problem. Some rather simple efforts by the universities might reestablish national faith in the higher education process. The question is whether the existing problems faced by higher education are an opportunity for change or a precursor to disaster. The pressures on higher education today provide institutions with the chance to reorganize and rededicate themselves so they can supply educated people who will contribute in a multitude of ways to the social well-being.

THE FOLLOW-UP SURVEY INSTRUMENT

DIRECTIONS: Your responses will be read by an optical mark reader. Your careful observance of these few simple rules will be most appreciated.

- Use only black lead pencil (No. 2 or less).
- Make heavy black marks that fill the circle.
- Erase cleanly any answer you wish to change.
- Make no stray markings of any kind.

EXAMPLE:

Will marks made with ball pen or fountain pen be properly read? Yes . ○   No . ●

1. Since you received your bachelor's degree, how many courses have you taken for graduate credit?
(Mark one)

○ None   ○ 1–3   ○ 4 or more

2. What is the highest degree you now hold? (Mark one)

○ Bachelor's
○ Master's
○ Doctorate or equivalent advanced degree
   (Ph.D., M.D., D.D.S., D.V.M., LL.B., etc.)

3. Using the following list of study areas, provide answers in columns A, B, and C as indicated:

Ⓐ In which area did you take the most courses for your undergraduate degree? (Mark one only)

   Ⓑ IF you attended graduate school, which is the area in which you took the most courses for credit? (Mark one)

      Ⓒ Which areas would you recommend as the most useful for someone preparing for a job like yours? (Mark all that apply)

Ⓐ Ⓑ Ⓒ English
Ⓐ Ⓑ Ⓒ Languages (Foreign)
Ⓐ Ⓑ Ⓒ Other Arts and Humanities (Fine Arts, Music, Philosophy, etc.)
Ⓐ Ⓑ Ⓒ Economics
Ⓐ Ⓑ Ⓒ Sociology
Ⓐ Ⓑ Ⓒ Psychology
Ⓐ Ⓑ Ⓒ History
Ⓐ Ⓑ Ⓒ Other Social Sciences (Anthropology, Geography, Political Science, etc.)
Ⓐ Ⓑ Ⓒ Biological Sciences
Ⓐ Ⓑ Ⓒ Mathematical Sciences
Ⓐ Ⓑ Ⓒ Chemistry, Biochemistry
Ⓐ Ⓑ Ⓒ Physics
Ⓐ Ⓑ Ⓒ Other Physical Sciences (Earth Sciences, etc.)
Ⓐ Ⓑ Ⓒ Accounting
Ⓐ Ⓑ Ⓒ Business Administration
Ⓐ Ⓑ Ⓒ Other Business
Ⓐ Ⓑ Ⓒ Architecture, Urban Planning
Ⓐ Ⓑ Ⓒ Education
Ⓐ Ⓑ Ⓒ Engineering
Ⓐ Ⓑ Ⓒ Other Fields (specify): _____

4. Looking back on your college education, please indicate the extent to which it has been useful in each of the following ways:
(Mark one for each line across)

	Very Much	Some-what	Not At All
It increased my general knowledge	Ⓥ	Ⓢ	Ⓝ
It increased my ability to think clearly	Ⓥ	Ⓢ	Ⓝ
It increased my leadership ability	Ⓥ	Ⓢ	Ⓝ
It taught me a skill that enabled me to get my first job	Ⓥ	Ⓢ	Ⓝ
It increased my chances of finding a good job	Ⓥ	Ⓢ	Ⓝ
It helped me choose my life goals	Ⓥ	Ⓢ	Ⓝ
It gave me knowledge and skills that I use in my current job	Ⓥ	Ⓢ	Ⓝ
My bachelor's degree was a factor in my being hired by my current employer	Ⓥ	Ⓢ	Ⓝ
My bachelor's degree was necessary to get promoted	Ⓥ	Ⓢ	Ⓝ
The contacts I made in college with professors or friends helped me get my current job	Ⓥ	Ⓢ	Ⓝ

5. Since you received your bachelor's degree, how many years have you been employed full time? (Mark one)

○ None   ○ Less than 2   ○ 2–4   ○ 5–7   ○ 8 or more

6. Are you employed at the present time? (Mark one)

○ Yes (full-time) ⎫
○ Yes (part-time) ⎬ GO TO QUESTION 8
○ No —— ANSWER QUESTION 7

7. IF YOU ARE NOT EMPLOYED:

a. When did you last hold a job? (Mark one)

○ Within the last 3 months   ○ Over a year ago
○ 4 – 12 months ago   ○ Never

b. Why are you not employed at the present time? (Mark all that apply)

○ Do not want to be employed at the present time
○ Enrolled in school
○ Traveling, vacationing for an extended time
○ Prefer volunteer or community activity
○ Would like to be employed, but am apprehensive about seeking employment
○ Would like a part-time job (or a job with flexible hours), but am unable to find one
○ Spouse discourages employment
○ Involved with home, child care (voluntarily)
○ Involved with home, child care because unable to find adequate substitute care
○ Not sure how to go about seeking employment
○ Am not seeking work because I feel that I would be unable to find a job
○ Am seeking work, but am unable to find a suitable job
○ Moved to a new location, haven't found a job
○ Was released from my job due to a company cut-back
○ Illness, accident, or health problems
○ Other (specify): _____

c. When do you plan to seek employment? (Mark one)

○ Am currently seeking employment
○ Within a year
○ 1 – 5 years from now
○ More than 5 years from now
○ Uncertain, but probably sometime in the future
○ Never

8. What is:

Ⓨ **Your current occupation?** (Mark one only)

Ⓢ Your **spouse's** occupation? (Mark one only)

- Ⓨ Ⓢ Accountant or financial analyst
- Ⓨ Ⓢ Administrative assistant or middle level office worker
- Ⓨ Ⓢ Administration – business
  (management at the executive level)
- Ⓨ Ⓢ Administration – education
  (superintendent, principal, etc.)
- Ⓨ Ⓢ Administration – government
  (manager, supervisor, etc.)
- Ⓨ Ⓢ Allied health (hygienist, lab technician, therapist, dietician, nurse, pharmacist, etc.)
- Ⓨ Ⓢ Architect or planner
- Ⓨ Ⓢ Business owner or proprietor
- Ⓨ Ⓢ Buyer or purchasing agent
- Ⓨ Ⓢ Clergy, religious worker
- Ⓨ Ⓢ Computer programmer
- Ⓨ Ⓢ Computer scientist, systems analyst
- Ⓨ Ⓢ Conservationist or forester
- Ⓨ Ⓢ Communications specialist (reporter, writer, T.V., advertising, public relations, etc.)
- Ⓨ Ⓢ Counselor (school, career, occupational, employment)
- Ⓨ Ⓢ Creative or performing artist
- Ⓨ Ⓢ Engineer
- Ⓨ Ⓢ Farmer or rancher
- Ⓨ Ⓢ Foreign service worker (including diplomat)
- Ⓨ Ⓢ Health professional (physician, dentist, optometrist, podiatrist, psychologist/analyst, veterinarian)
- Ⓨ Ⓢ Librarian
- Ⓨ Ⓢ Law enforcement worker
- Ⓨ Ⓢ Lawyer (attorney)

- Ⓨ Ⓢ Mathematician, statistician, or actuary
- Ⓨ Ⓢ Military service
- Ⓨ Ⓢ Sales or broker
- Ⓨ Ⓢ Scientist – biological, physical, natural
- Ⓨ Ⓢ Scientist – social
- Ⓨ Ⓢ Secretary or clerk
- Ⓨ Ⓢ Social welfare or community worker
- Ⓨ Ⓢ Teacher (elementary or secondary)
- Ⓨ Ⓢ Teacher or professor (at college, university, or other post-secondary institution)
- Ⓨ Ⓢ Technician
- Ⓨ Ⓢ Transportation worker
- Ⓨ Ⓢ Skilled worker (or apprentice)
- Ⓨ Ⓢ Semi-skilled worker
- Ⓨ Ⓢ Unskilled laborer
- Ⓨ Ⓢ Other (specify): _____

- Ⓢ Not employed (housewife, volunteer worker, etc.)

9. At what point in your life did you select your current occupation?
(Mark one)

- ◯ Before entering college
- ◯ During college
- ◯ Around graduation time
- ◯ Within 5 years after graduation
- ◯ More recently

10. Which category best describes the type of organization in which you are employed? (Mark one)

- ◯ Commerce, finance, insurance, real estate
- ◯ Manufacturing or construction
- ◯ Retail or wholesale trade
- ◯ Transportation or public utilities
- ◯ Agriculture or mining
- ◯ College, university, technical institute or professional school
- ◯ Elementary or secondary school system
- ◯ Other business or service establishments
- ◯ Human services organization (social welfare, health, etc.)
- ◯ U.S. military service, active duty, or Commission Corps
- ◯ U.S. government, civilian employee
- ◯ State, local, or other government
- ◯ Other (specify): _____

11. Approximately how many persons does your company or organization employ? (Mark one)

- ◯ I work alone
- ◯ Less than 10
- ◯ 10 – 49
- ◯ 50 – 199
- ◯ 200 – 999
- ◯ 1,000 – 4,999
- ◯ 5,000 – 9,999
- ◯ 10,000 – 24,999
- ◯ 25,000 or more

| QUESTION 12 |

12. Mark **all** work activities that:

Ⓐ You now perform on your job

Ⓑ Your college education prepared you to perform (whether or not you perform them on your job)

Ⓒ You would like to do but are not now doing

- Ⓐ Ⓑ Ⓒ Accounting
- Ⓐ Ⓑ Ⓒ Administration, management
- Ⓐ Ⓑ Ⓒ Clerical
- Ⓐ Ⓑ Ⓒ Counseling
- Ⓐ Ⓑ Ⓒ Data processing, computer science
- Ⓐ Ⓑ Ⓒ Engineering
- Ⓐ Ⓑ Ⓒ Farming or forestry
- Ⓐ Ⓑ Ⓒ Health service
- Ⓐ Ⓑ Ⓒ Mathematical, statistical, actuarial
- Ⓐ Ⓑ Ⓒ Performing or creative arts
- Ⓐ Ⓑ Ⓒ Personnel, employee relations
- Ⓐ Ⓑ Ⓒ Production, quality control
- Ⓐ Ⓑ Ⓒ Program planning or budgeting
- Ⓐ Ⓑ Ⓒ Promotion, public relations, advertising
- Ⓐ Ⓑ Ⓒ Publications
- Ⓐ Ⓑ Ⓒ Public safety, law enforcement, community service work
- Ⓐ Ⓑ Ⓒ Research (laboratory)
- Ⓐ Ⓑ Ⓒ Research (other)
- Ⓐ Ⓑ Ⓒ Sales or marketing
- Ⓐ Ⓑ Ⓒ Speaking to groups, discussion leading
- Ⓐ Ⓑ Ⓒ Teaching
- Ⓐ Ⓑ Ⓒ Technological design or construction
- Ⓐ Ⓑ Ⓒ Technology (other)
- Ⓐ Ⓑ Ⓒ Training
- Ⓐ Ⓑ Ⓒ Writing, editing
- Ⓐ Ⓑ Ⓒ Other (specify): _____

13. How long have you been with this same employer? (Mark one)

- ◯ Less than 1 year
- ◯ Between 1 and 2 years
- ◯ Between 2 and 3 years
- ◯ More than 3 years

14. How satisfied are you with your current job?
(Mark one)

- ◯ Very satisfied
- ◯ Somewhat satisfied
- ◯ Not at all satisfied

15. How frequently do you use each of the following aspects of your college education in your current job?

(Mark one for each line across)

	Almost Always	Frequently	Sometimes	Rarely	Never
I use the content of courses in my undergraduate major field	◯	◯	◯	◯	◯
I use the content of courses in my undergraduate minor field	◯	◯	◯	◯	◯
I use the content of other undergraduate courses	◯	◯	◯	◯	◯
I use the content of courses taken for graduate credit	◯	◯	◯	◯	◯

16. How closely related is your job to your undergraduate major field? (Mark one)

○ Closely related —— Go to QUESTION 17
○ Somewhat related ─┐
○ Not related ────────┴─ **CONTINUE**

Why are you working in a job only "somewhat" or "not" related to your undergraduate major? (Mark all that apply)

○ Never planned to take a closely related job
○ Prefer line of work not closely related
○ Tried closely related employment, but did not like it
○ First job was unrelated to major field and I became interested in this type of work
○ Joined family business or firm
○ Found a better paying job
○ Found a job that offers a better chance for career advancement
○ No longer in closely related job due to promotion
○ Wanted part-time work, flexible hours
○ Wanted to work at home
○ Am on a temporary assignment (VISTA, Peace Corps, USIA, foreign service, missionary work, etc.)
○ Jobs related to major are not available where I live and I do not want to move
○ Am in the military
○ Could not get a closely related job, but would prefer one
○ Limited in job selection by situation of spouse, family responsibilities
○ Very few jobs are related to my major
○ Employment opportunities are scarce for people in jobs related to my major

17. Aside from your college education, how did you acquire the knowledge or skills necessary for your job? (Mark all that apply)

○ Formal training at an outside institution
○ Company (or in-house) formal training program
○ On-the-job training
○ Picked it up myself
○ No training required

18. Indicate whether each of the following statements is correct in reference to your current job: (Mark all that apply)

○ I supervise people trained in my field of study
○ I am well paid for my work compared with persons of the same job level in my place of employment
○ I am well paid for my work compared with persons at the same job level in other work settings
○ I am well paid for my work compared with people in general with the same amount of education
○ Most of my colleagues are trained in my field of study
○ Most of the time I set my own work hours
○ Most of the time I design my own program of work
○ I have policy and decision-making responsibility
○ I am satisfied with the quality of interaction with my supervisor
○ I have sufficient status or prestige in my job
○ I am satisfied with my career progress to date
○ My current job offers good future prospects for further advancement
○ My job fits my long-range goals
○ I would like to remain with my current employer for the foreseeable future
○ My skills are fully utilized in my job
○ I am working at a professional level
○ During college I had a part-time or summer job related to my current job
○ I am self employed

19. What is your current annual salary before taxes? (If self-employed, indicate your annual earned income after adjusting for business expenses) (Mark one)

○ None   ○ $17,000 – 19,999
○ Below $7,000   ○ $20,000 – 24,999
○ $7,000 – 9,999   ○ $25,000 – 29,999
○ $10,000 – 11,999   ○ $30,000 – 34,999
○ $12,000 – 13,999   ○ $35,000 – 39,999
○ $14,000 – 16,999   ○ $40,000 and over

20. How many other full-time jobs (with different employers) have you held since you graduated from college? (Mark one)

○ None (same employer since graduation)
○ Have held one other job
○ Have held 2 – 3 other jobs
○ Have held 4 or more other jobs

21. Were any of your previous jobs closely related to your undergraduate major?

○ Yes   ○ No

22. What is your sex?

○ Male   ○ Female

23. What is your current marital status? (Mark one)

○ Single (never married)
○ Married
○ Separated, divorced, widowed

24. Are you: (Mark all that apply)

○ White/Caucasian
○ Black/Negro/Afro-American
○ American Indian
○ Oriental
○ Mexican-American/Chicano
○ Puerto Rican-American
○ Other

THANK YOU FOR YOUR COOPERATION

Return your questionnaire to:
HIGHER EDUCATION RESEARCH INSTITUTE
c/o Intran Processing Center
4555 West 77th Street
Minneapolis, Minnesota 55435

169

APPENDIX B

ADDITIONAL TABLES

TABLE B.1

Selection of Relationship-Defining Variables

Variable	Reason for Selection
1. Degree to which respondent uses the content of his major courses on the job	Had significant entering and final F values in original regression
2. Whether respondent works with colleagues trained in his field	Were not significantly correlated with each other and with other relationship-defining variables
3. Whether respondent recommends his major to someone preparing for his job	Were significantly correlated with dependent variable, relation of job to major
4. Whether respondent indicates his college education provided him with knowledge useful in his current job	
5. "Useless"—the number of activities for which college trained the respondent but which he is not using on his current job	Had significant entering and final F values in original regression
6. Degree to which respondent uses the content of other (nonmajor) courses in his job	Were not significantly correlated with other relationship-defining variables
7. Whether respondents supervised people trained in his field	
8. Whether college training gave respondent the ability to think clearly	Was significantly correlated with other variables (such as those indicating that college education trained respondent in leadership and provided general knowledge), thus courses fully representing that section of the relationship variables

Note: Omitted variables were indications of whether the respondents thought their college education provided them with a skill useful in their first job, because the interest of this study was primarily in the current job, which was not necessarily the first one. Moreover, the correlation ($r = .44$) was significant (at the .01 level) between the responses that college education provided skills for a first job and knowledge useful in the current job. Also excluded was the share of activities currently performed for which college education trained a respondent, because this variable was computed from the same set of responses that yielded "useless," and the latter was included in the regression.

Further excluded were variables indicating that college education provided the respondent with general knowledge, chances for a good job, and help in selecting life goals, and that the bachelor's degree was a factor in being hired, because these variables were highly intercorrelated. All were significantly correlated with the indication that college education provided the individual with knowledge useful in his current job. An indication that skills were fully utilized on the job was not selected as an explanatory variable since it had neither a significant entering nor a final F value. However, the skills fully utilized variable included in the regression in Table 6.3 was significant in explaining relationship for five specific occupations.

TABLE B.2

Simple Correlations of Relationship Variables with Relation of Job to Major

Variable	Correlation with Relation of Job to Major
Relationship defining	
Use content of major courses	.73[b]
Colleagues trained in my field	.36[b]
Recommend major as preparation for job	.34[b]
College provided knowledge and skills used in current job	.51[b]
Number of work activities college prepared but which I do not do	−.15
Use content of other undergraduate courses	.16
Supervise people trained in my field	.20[a]
College increased ability to think clearly	−.01
Other relationship variables	
College increased my general knowledge	−.02
College increased my leadership ability	.12
College taught skill which helped me get my first job	.43[b]
College increased my chances for finding a good job	.25[b]
College helped me choose my life goals	.27[b]
B.A. was a factor in hiring	.27[b]
B.A. was necessary for promotion	.18
College provided contacts which helped me get current job	.17
Number of activities college prepared me to do	.21[a]
Proportion of activities I do which college prepared me to do	.39[b]
Number of work activities I do	−.04

[a]Significant at .05 level.
[b]Significant at .01 level.

TABLE B.3

Intercorrelations of Relationship Variables

Variable	1	2	3	4	5	6	7	8	9	10	11	12	13	14	15	16	17	18	19	20
1. Relation of job to major	1.0																			
2. Use content of major courses in my job	.73[b]	1.0																		
3. Use content of other undergraduate courses	.16	.30[b]	1.0																	
4. Recommend major as preparation for job	.34[b]	.29[b]	.04	1.0																
5. College taught knowledge and skills used in current job	.51[b]	.56[b]	.26[b]	.25[b]	1.0															
6. Number of work activities college prepared but not doing	-.15	-.09	.02	-.04	-.06	1.0														
7. Colleagues are in my field	.36[b]	.27[b]	.10	.13	.24[a]	-.09	1.0													
8. Supervise people in my field	.20[a]	.16	.04	.11	.16	-.03	.18	1.0												
9. College increased my ability to think clearly	-.01	.05	.08	.00	.08	.04	.01	.03	1.0											
10. College increased general knowledge	-.02	.07	.11	.02	.12	.04	-.01	-.02	.28[b]	1.0										

172

	1	2	3	4	5	6	7	8	9	10	11	12	13	14	15	16	17	18	19	20
11. College increased leadership ability	.12	.17	.13	.01	.19	.02	.07	.06	.30[b]	.13	1.0									
12. College taught skill which enabled me to get my first job	.43[b]	.42[b]	.17	.12	.44[b]	-.04	.28[b]	.08	.05	.06	.17	1.0								
13. College increased my chances of finding a good job	.25[b]	.24[b]	.11	.13	.30[b]	-.03	.17	.08	.09	.08	.12	.17	1.0							
14. College helped me choose my life goals	.27[b]	.29[b]	.14	.10	.36[b]	-.00	.16	.06	.20[a]	.14	.26[b]	.12	.41[b]	1.0						
15. B.A. was a factor in my being hired	.27[b]	.22[a]	.08	.17	.37[b]	-.05	.23[a]	.12	.03	.01	.07	.34[b]	.27[b]	.27[b]	1.0					
16. B.A. was necessary for promotion	.18	.17	.10	.14	.25[b]	-.02	.18	.15	.06	.04	.07	.28[b]	.28[b]	.38[b]	.48[b]	1.0				
17. College provided contacts for current job	.17	.18	.11	.05	.19	-.00	.11	.05	.03	.03	.11	.19	.19	.27[b]	.19	.16	1.0			
18. Number of work activities college prepared	.21[a]	.24[a]	.16	.11	.20[a]	.12	.07	.19	.06	.04	.06	.15	.10	.10	.12	.08	.14	1.0		
19. Number of work activities I do	-.04	.00	.05	.02	.03	.13	-.04	.22[a]	.01	.00	.05	.11	.10	-.02	.08	.10	.07	.66[b]	1.0	
20. Proportion of work activities I do which college prepared	.39[b]	.37[b]	.14	.16	.28[b]	.06	.21[a]	-.00	.03	.03	.13	.27[b]	.17	.19	.13	.10		.54[b]	.04	1.0

[a] Significant at .05 level.
[b] Significant at .01 level.

TABLE B.4

Increments in R^2s for Job Satisfaction and Income Regressions, Run Three Ways, by Total and Sex

Regression	Total		Men		Women	
	Background	Relationship	Background	Relationship	Background	Relationship
Job satisfaction						
With relation of job to major	.057	.063	.067	.072	.060	.066
With voluntary/involuntary variables	.057	.097	.068	.098	.059	.108
With defining variables	.046	.067	.060	.077	.047	.081
Income						
With relation of job to major	.406	.406	.206	.206	.347	.348
With voluntary/involuntary variables	.406	.414	.207	.215	.345	.364
With defining variables	.383	.400	.202	.229	.347	.359

Ash, P. 1972. Job satisfaction differences among women of different ethnic groups. *Journal of Vocational Behavior* 2, no. 4: 495–507.

Astin, A. W. 1971. *Predicting academic performance in college.* New York: Free Press.

Astin, A. W., and Panos, R. J. 1969. *The educational and vocational development of college students.* Washington: American Council on Education.

Astin, A. W., et al. 1974. *The American freshman: National norms for fall 1974.* Los Angeles: University of California.

———. 1975. *The American freshman: National norms for fall 1975.* Los Angeles: University of California.

Berg, I. 1971. *Education and jobs: The great training robbery.* Boston: Beacon Press.

Bird, C., and Boyer, E. 1975. Is college necessary? *Change* 7, no. 1: 32–37.

Bisconti, A. S. 1974. The new college freshman: Signs of change (trends on the plans and goals of freshmen, 1966–1973). *Update* 1.

———. 1975. *College graduates and the employers—A national study of career plans and their outcomes.* Bethlehem, Pennsylvania: CPC Foundation.

Bisconti, A. S., and Astin, H. A. 1973. *Undergraduate and graduate study in scientific fields.* Washington, D.C.: ACE Research Reports 8, no. 3.

Bisconti, A. S., and Gomberg, I. K. 1975a. *The hard-to-place majority.* Bethlehem, Pennsylvania: CPC Foundation.

———. 1975b. *Careers in the private sector—A national study of college graduates in business and industry.* Bethlehem, Pennsylvania: CPC Foundation.

Bisconti, A. S., and Solmon, L. C. 1974. *The invisible scholars: Where have all the bachelors gone?* Washington: National Research Council.

———. 1976. *College education on the job—The graduates' viewpoint.* Bethlehem, Pennsylvania: College Placement Council.

Bowen, H. R. 1974. Higher education: A growth industry? *Educational Record* 55, no. 3: 147–58.

Brayfield, A. H.; Wells, R. V.; and Strats, M. W. 1957. Interrationships among measures of job satisfaction and general satisfaction. *Journal of Applied Psychology* 41: 201–05.

Bureau of Labor Statistics. 1974. *Occupational outlook handbook,* Washington: Government Printing Office.

————. 1974. The unemployed and the underemployed. *Vocational Guidance Quarterly* 22: 170–71.

Campbell, D. P. and Klein, K. L. 1975. Job satisfaction and vocational interests. *Vocational Guidance Quarterly* 24: 125–31.

Carnegie Commission on Higher Education. 1973. *College graduates and jobs: Adjusting to a new labor market situation.* New York: McGraw-Hill.

Cherry, N. 1975. Occupational values and employment: A follow-up study of graduate men and women. *Higher Education* 4: 357–68.

Chiswick, B. R. 1973. Schooling, screening, and income. In *Does College Matter?,* eds. L. C. Solmon and P. J. Taubman. New York: Academic Press.

A culture in transformation: Toward a different societal ethic? 1975. TAP Report 12. New York: Institute of Life Insurance.

Davis, L. E. 1972. Quality of working life: National and international developments. Proceedings of the twenty-fifth annual meeting, Madison, Wisconsin: Industrial Relations Research Association.

DePauw Alumnus. 1975. Careers: Putting the B.A. to work. October 1975, pp. 8–9.

Dresch, S. P. 1975. Education saturation: A demographic-economic model. *AAUP Bulletin,* October 1975, pp. 239–47.

Dumazedier, J., and Latouche, N. 1962. Work and leisure in French sociology. *Industrial Relations* 1: 13–30.

El-Khawas, E. H., and Bisconti, A. S. 1974. *Five and ten years after college entry.* Washington: American Council on Education.

Flanders, R. B. 1970. Employment patterns for the 1970s. *Occupational Outlook Quarterly* 14: 2–7.

Fogel, W., and Mitchell, D. F. B. 1974. Higher education decision making and the labor market. In *Higher Education and the Labor Market,* ed. M. S. Gordon. New York: McGraw-Hill, 1974.

Freeman, R., and Hollomon, J. H. 1975. "The declining value of college going." *Change* 7, no. 7: 24–31, 62.

Ginzberg, E. 1972. Toward a theory of occupational choice: A restatement. *Vocational Guidance Quarterly* 20, no. 3: 169–76.

Gordon, M. S., ed. 1974. *Higher education and the labor market.* New York: McGraw-Hill.

————. 1975. The labor market and student interests. *Liberal Education* 61, no. 2: 149–60.

Gottlieb, D. 1975. College youth and the meaning of work. *Vocational Guidance Quarterly* 24: 116–24.

Greenhaus, J. H. 1974. Career salience as a moderator of the relationship between satisfaction with occupational preference and satisfaction with life in general. *Journal of Psychology* 86, no. 1: 53–55.

Grubb, W. N., and Lazerson, M. 1975. Rally 'round the workplace: Continuities and fallacies in career education. *Harvard Educational Review* 45, no. 4: 451–74.

Handa, M. L., and Skolnik, M. L. 1975. Unemployment, expected returns, and the demand for university education in Ontario: Some empirical results. *Higher Education* 4: 27–43.

Hauser, P. M. 1975. "Education and careers—Concordant or discordant?" Address at the College Placement Council National Meeting, Washington, D.C., May 27–30, 1975.

Henle, P. 1975. Worker dissatisfaction: A look at the economic effects. *Vocational Guidance Quarterly* 24: 152–54.

Hoppock, R. 1975. Reminiscences and comments on job satisfaction. *Vocational Guidance Quarterly* 24: 107–15.

Hoyt, K. 1974. *Career education, vocational education, and occupational education: An approach to defining differences.* Columbus, Ohio: Center for Vocational Education, Ohio State University.

————. 1975. Untitled address at the College Placement Council National Meeting, Washington, D.C., May 27–30, 1975.

Iris, B., and Barrett, G. V. 1972. Some relations between job and life satisfaction and job importance. *Journal of Applied Psychology* 56: 301–04.

Kaplan, H. R. 1975. How do workers view their work in America? *Vocational Guidance Quarterly* 24: 165–68.

Kohn, M. L., and Schooler, C. 1973. Occupational experience and psychological functioning: An assessment of reciprocal effects. *American Sociological Review* 38, no. 1: 97–118.

Kornhauser, A. 1965. *Mental health of the industrial worker.* New York: Wiley.

Levihan, S. A., and Johnson, W. B. 1975. Job redesign, reform, enrichment—Exploring the limitations. *Vocational Guidance Quarterly* 24: 172–80.

McCrea, J. 1974. The college student's occupational outlook. *Rocky Mountain Social Science Journal* 11, no. 3: 27–36.

Mincer, J. 1970. The determination of labor incomes: A survey with special reference to the human capital approach. *Journal of Economic Literature* 8: 1–26.

National Institute of Education. 1974. *Career education program: Program plan for fiscal year 1975.* Washington: Department of Health, Education and Welfare.

Newman, F. 1975. Untitled address at the College Placement Council National Meeting, Washington, D.C., May 27–30.

O'Hara, J. G. 1975. Untitled address at the College Placement Council National Meeting, Washington, D.C., May 27–30.

O'Toole, J. 1975. The reserve army of the underemployed. *Change* 7, no. 4: 26–33, 63; no. 5: 26–33, 60–62.

Quinn, R., and Cobb, W., Jr. 1971. *What workers want: Factor analyses of importance ratings of job facets.* Ann Arbor, Michigan: Survey Research Center.

Quinn, R. P. and de Mandilovitch, M. S. 1975. *Education and job satisfaction: A questionable payoff.* Ann Arbor, Michigan: Survey Research Center, University of Michigan.

Quinn, R., and Mangione, T. W. 1973. Evaluating weighted models of measuring job satisfaction: A Cinderella story. *Organizational Behavior and Human Performance* 10, no. 1: 1–23.

Quinn, R., and Shepard, L. J. 1974. *The 1972–73 quality of employment survey.* Ann Arbor, Michigan: Survey of Research Center, Institute for Social Research, University of Michigan.

Rawlins, V. L., and Ulman, L. 1974. The utilization of college-trained manpower in the United States. In *Higher Education and the Labor Market,* ed. M. S. Gordon. New York: McGraw-Hill, 1974.

Sarason, S. B.; Sarason, E. K.; and Cowden, P. 1975. Aging and the nature of work. *American Psychologist* 30, no. 5: 584–92.

Slim pickings for the class of '76. 1976. *Time,* March 29, pp. 46–49.

Solmon, L. C. 1975. The definition of college quality and its impact on earnings. *Explorations in Economic Research 1975* 2, no. 4: 537–87.

Solmon, L. C., and Taubman, P. J. 1973. *Does college matter?* New York: Academic Press.

Taubman, P., and Wales, T. 1975. Education as an investment and a screening device. In *Education, Income, and Human Behavior,* ed. F. T. Juster. New York: McGraw-Hill, 1975.

Toombs, W. 1973. *The Comm-Bacc study: Postbaccalaureate activities of degree recipients from Pennsylvania institutions 1971–1972.* University Park, Pennsylvania: Center for the Study of Higher Education, Pennsylvania State University.

Tussing, A. D. 1975. Emergence of the new unemployment. *Intellect* 103: 303–11.

UCLA Institute of Industrial Relations. 1974. Job satisfaction: Issues and criteria. Presentations to the sixteenth annual research conference, "Changing World of Work." University of California, Los Angeles.

U.S. Department of Health, Education, and Welfare. 1973. *Work in America.* Cambridge, Massachusetts: MIT Press.

U.S. Department of Labor. 1972. *Manpower report of the president: Transmitted to Congress, March 1972.* Washington, D.C.

———. 1974. Job satisfaction: Is there a trend? *Manpower Research Monograph,* no. 30.

Warren, J. R. 1975. The match between higher education and occupations. In *Responding to changing human resource needs,* eds. P. Heist and J. R. Warren. San Francisco: Jossey-Bass.

Weaver, C. N. 1974. Correlates of job satisfaction: Some evidence from the national surveys. *Academy of Management Journal* 17, no. 2: 373–75.

———. 1975. Job preferences of white collar and blue collar workers. *Academy of Management Journal* 18, no. 1: 167–75.

Wirty, W., et al. 1975. *The boundless resource: A prospective for an education-work policy.* Washington: New Republic Book Company.

Wool, H. 1975. What's wrong with work in America?—A review essay. *Vocational Guidance Quarterly* 24: 155–64.

LEWIS C. SOLMON was born in Toronto, Canada, in 1942. He received his B.Com. from the University of Toronto in 1964 and his Ph.D. in Economics from the University of Chicago in 1968. Currently, he is Executive Officer of the Higher Education Research Institute in Los Angeles and Associate Professor in Residence at the Graduate School of Education, University of California at Los Angeles. He has taught at Purdue University, City University of New York, and Virginia Polytechnic Institute and State University, and has been a Research Fellow and Research Associate at the National Bureau of Economic Research.

His books include *Economics; Does College Matter?; Male and Female Graduate Students: The Question of Equal Opportunity;* and *Capital Formation by Expenditures on Formal Education, 1880 and 1890.* He has published numerous articles in professional journals of economics and education, and has served on a number of national advisory panels dealing with education and career development.

ANN S. BISCONTI is a social psychologist whose broad survey research experience ranges from market research to studies of human resource development. In recent years, a main study interest has been the educational and career progress of college students, particularly the relationships between education and work. Among her numerous publications are the two books *Higher Education and the Disadvantaged Student* and *The Power of Protest.* A Research Associate at the Higher Education Research Institute and Research Coordinator at University Research Corporation (on leave), she is currently residing in Italy where she is engaged in a study of community participation in governance of the public schools.

NANCY L. OCHSNER received her B.A. in Psychology from DePauw University, Indiana, in 1972, and her M.A. in Education from the University of California at Riverside, in 1975. She is currently a Research Analyst at the Higher Education Research Institute in Los Angeles. Previously she held research assistantships at the University of California and at Geisinger Medical Center, Danville, Pennsylvania.

RELATED TITLES

Published by

Praeger Special Studies

ACADEMIC GAMESMANSHIP: Student-Oriented
Change in Higher Education

Alexander W. Astin

CRISES IN CAMPUS MANAGEMENT: Case Studies in
the Administration of Colleges and Universities

edited by
George J. Mauer

MALE AND FEMALE GRADUATE STUDENTS: The
Question of Equal Opportunity

Lewis C. Solmon

MINORITIES IN U.S. INSTITUTIONS OF HIGHER
EDUCATION

Frank Brown
Madelon D. Stent

OCCUPATIONAL CHOICES AND TRAINING
NEEDS: Prospects for the 1980s

Leonard A. Lecht

PLURALISM IN A DEMOCRATIC SOCIETY

edited by
Melvin M. Tumin
Walter Plotch

THE WORLD'S STUDENTS IN THE UNITED
STATES: A Review and Evaluation of Research on
Foreign Students

Seth Spaulding
Michael Flack